POCKET

BRUGES & BRUSSELS

TOP SIGHTS · LOCAL EXPERIENCES

BENEDICT WALKER, HELENA SMITH

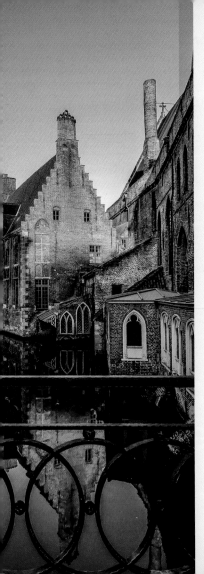

Contents

Plan Your Trip

Bruges at sunset
JESS LAUER/GETTY IMAGES ©

Welcome to Bruges & Brussels

The Bs have it: romantic, canal-woven Bruges and buzzing multinational Brussels are Belgium's unmissable duo. While Brussels dwarfs Bruges in size, both feature boats plying waterways, serene parks, a web of cycling trails, lively marketplaces, forward-looking fashion and galleries packed with home-grown art, from Brueghel masterpieces to Hergé's Tintin. All this plus the finest beer and chocolate in the world.

Grand Place (p80), Brussels
HECTOR CHRISTIAEN/SHUTTERSTOCK ©

Top Sights

Markt

Magnificent, magical, medieval square at the heart of Bruges. **p36**

Burg

Bruges' eclectic architecture hub.
p38

Begijnhof

A prayerful place of peace in Bruges.
p60

Grand Place

Europe's most theatrical medieval square, in Brussels.
p80

Groeningemuseum

Bruges' best fine art collection. **p56**

Museum Sint-Janshospitaal

Memling and medicine, Bruges. **p58**

Parc du Cinquantenaire

Green space and Brussels culture. **p126**

Musée Art & Histoire

World cultures on display in Brussels. **p128**

Centre Belge de la Bande Dessinée

Lively comics in Brussels. **p82**

Musées Royaux des Beaux-Arts

Old and new art in Brussels. **p108**

MIM

Magical sounds and marvellous architecture in Brussels. **p110**

Musée Horta

Brussels' greatest art nouveau creation. **p138**

Eating

Bring a healthy appetite with you – restaurants in Bruges and Brussels dish up a seemingly endless procession of delicious fare. What's more, Belgium boasts more Michelin stars per capita than anywhere else in Europe. Many cafés (bars and pubs) also serve hearty meals.

What to Eat

Breakfast in Flanders is a hearty affair of cured meats, cheeses, cereals and so on. At lunchtime many restaurants offer a dish of the day (*dagschotel* in Dutch; *plat du jour* in French). Also watch for a 'menu of the day' (*dagmenu; menu du jour*). These set menus comprise three or more courses and work out cheaper than ordering individual courses à la carte. Some kitchens open as early as 6pm for dinner, but most don't get busy until at least a couple of hours later.

Mussels & Frites

If Belgium has a national dish, it is mussels (*mosselen* in Dutch; *moules* in French). Forget about using a fork to scoop out these much-loved molluscs; use an empty shell as a pincer to prise them out. Fries (*frieten* or *frites*) are even more ubiquitous. Not only do they accompany mussels (and virtually any other dish), but they are easily Belgium's favourite snack.

Meat Lovers

Those of a delicate disposition, beware: Belgians' idea of *saignant* (rare) meat drips with blood; *à point* (medium) is what other nationalities consider rare, and *bien cuit* is the closest you'll get to well done (these French terms are also used by Dutch speakers). *Bleu* steaks will barely have bounced off the grill.

Best Belgian Food, Bruges

Lieven Book ahead for this extremely popular Belgian bistro. (p46)

LUNCH

SOUPE A L'OIGNON
ꝰ
OEUF DUR MOUTARDE
ꝰ
1 FONDU AU FROMAGE
ꝰ
SALADE AUX LARDONS
✦
FILET DE PANGAS HOMARDIN
ꝰ
BOULETTES BRUXELLOISES
ꝰ
STEAK DE DINDE ARCHIDUC
ꝰ
SAUCISSE STOEMP
✦
GLACE VANILLE
ꝰ
MOUSSE AU CHOCOLAT
ꝰ
CREME CARAMEL

STUART FORSTER/ALAMY STOCK PHOTO ©

Den Dyver A pioneer of fine beer dining. (p69)

Pomperlut Great food with a fine terrace and cosy dark-wood interior. (p69)

Best Belgian Food, Brussels

Chez Léon (pictured) Long-time tourist fave known for its 'Mussels from Brussels' (p93)

L'Idiot du Village Book ahead for tables at this colourful, cosy restaurant. (p117)

In 't Spinnekopke A lovely old cottage restaurant serving up meaty Belgian specials. (p93)

Best Seafood

De Stove A 20-seat gem where fish caught daily is the house speciality. (Bruges; p46)

Bij den Boer This convivial fish restaurant won't break the bank. (Brussels; p93)

Mer du Nord Sublime scampi from one of the city's best fishmonger windows. (Brussels; p90)

Best Comfort Food

Charli Bargain pastries and cakes made with organic ingredients. (Brussels; p92)

Maison Antoine Brussels' best *frites*? You decide. (Brussels; p133)

That's Toast The one and only for all-day breakfasts. (Bruges; p46)

Traditional Belgian Dishes

Bloedworst Pig's blood black pudding, with apple sauce

Paardenfilet/steack de cheval Horse steak

Filet américain Minced beef served raw

Konijn met pruimen Tender rabbit in prune sauce

Drinking & Nightlife

You'll encounter a bewildering choice of Belgian beers and jenevers (gin) at just about every drinking establishment. In bars and clubs, jazz is the style of live music you'll encounter most often. Look out for flyers in music shops, street-wear boutiques, bars and cafés about DJ nights, club fixtures and one-off parties.

Drinking Culture

At specialised drinking establishments, you'll be handed a thick menu detailing hundreds of varieties. Wading through the menus is a Herculean feat: ask the staff for the flavours and characteristics you have in mind and be guided by them. Drinking establishments usually open around 10am; closing hours aren't restricted by law but simply depend on how busy it is on the night.

Everyone buys rounds, except 'Bob' – the Belgian name for the designated driver.

Remember to say 'cheers!' – in Dutch, *schol* (or *gezondheid* – 'to your health'), and in French, *santé!*

All Kinds of Watering Holes

Cafés always serve alcohol and some, though not all, also serve food. Places that do are sometimes classified as an *eet-café* (eating cafe) or a *grand café* (a larger, more elegant version of an *eetcafé*), and it's fine to just stop in for a drink even if you're not dining. You can

also just pop in for a drink at a brasserie or bistro, although these are chiefly eateries. Anywhere that labels itself a bar generally only serves drinks. Likewise, a *herberg* (Dutch for 'tavern') is primarily a drinking spot. One of the most atmospheric *cafés* for drinking is the traditional *bruin café* ('brown cafe', sometimes called a *bruine kroeg*). So named for their wood panelling, interspersed with oversized mirrors, these small, cosy, old-fashioned pubs are prime places for mixing with locals.

MARTINA BADINI/SHUTTERSTOCK ©

Best Specialist Beer Pubs, Bruges

Herberg Vlissinghe The city's oldest bar is not to be missed. (p48)

De Garre Brace your tastebuds for 11% Garre beer. (p48)

't Poatersgat Cellar bar with umpteen Trappist beers to sample. (p48)

Best Specialist Beer Pubs, Brussels

À la Mort Subite (pictured) Come for the unchanged decor and vibe. (p96)

La Fleur en Papier Doré The walls feature scribbles by surrealist Brussels homeboy Magritte. (p95)

Brussels Beer Project One of the most innovative players in the Brussels' beer scene. (p94)

Best Live Music Bars

Du Phare Blues and jazz venue at the north end of town. (Bruges; p50)

Le Cercle des Voyageurs Piano jazz and experimental music near Grand Place. (Brussels; p91)

Walvis From soul to punk to progressive rock, live acts and DJ sets. (Brussels; p95)

Best Drinking Vibes

De Stoepa A fabulous summer courtyard for drinks or dinner too, near the station. (Bruges; p69)

BarBeton Aperitivos, cocktail hours and DJ nights. (Brussels; p94)

Goupil le Fol Overwhelming weirdness in a sensory overload of rambling passageways. (Brussels; p93)

Shopping

Beer and chocolate top most shopping lists for visitors to Bruges and Brussels, and each city has an astonishing array of both. Other unique buys include handmade lace, designer fashions, classic comics, diamonds and quality antiques. Bargain hunters should visit during the two annual sales periods – the first week of January and July.

Chocolate

Glinting light-brown, dark-brown and creamy-white coated squares, oblongs, balls and cups, embossed gold stamps and elaborate swirls, wrapped in shimmering tinfoil or twisted inside cellophane. Yes, even shopping for chocolate is an art in Belgium – and it would want to be, with premium chocolates reaching €120 per kilogram. A turning point for Belgian chocolate came in 1912, when pralines (filled chocolates) were created in Brussels. Today these are undergoing another evolution at the hands of Belgium's mould-breaking chocolatiers, whose fusion pralines incorporate flavours such as Havana cigar, cauliflower, green pea, chilli and wasabi.

Where to Buy Chocolate

In addition to the rarefied showrooms of top chocolatiers, there are also numerous luxury chains. Popular local manufacturers include Leonidas, the original praline creator Neuhaus and Galler, which also offers its superb pralines (such as fresh pistachio-filled white chocolate) in bar form.

Best Fashion & Vintage

Stijl The Antwerp Six designers are showcased here. (Brussels; p101)

Gabriele High-class vintage gear to brighten up your look. (Brussels; p98)

Oliver Strelli Home to one of Belgium's top designers. (Bruges; p53)

BOTOND HORVATH/SHUTTERSTOCK ©

Best for Chocolate

Galler Heaven for chocaholics, just off Markt. (Bruges; p52)

Chocolate Line Wildly experimental flavours by 'shock-o-latier' Dominique Persoone. (Bruges; p52)

Mary Pick a praline or have some boxed up to take home. (Brussels; p99)

Neuhaus The original – established in 1857. (Brussels; p100)

Best Food & Drink

Pierre Marcolini Sumptuous treats, some made with Cuban chocolate. (Brussels; p121)

Zucchero Make a beeline to this confectioner if you prefer candy to chocolate. (Bruges; p73)

De Biertempel The place to buy your beer-related gifts. (Brussels; p100)

Best Bookshops

Passa Porta A meeting point for literary types in the city. (Brussels; p99)

Tropismes (pictured) Gorgeous bookshop in the swish Galerie des Princes. (Brussels; p101)

De Reyghere Reisboek-handel Possibly the world's best travel bookshop. (Bruges; p52)

Tip for Buying Chocolate

You'll find many top chain brands in supermarkets for a fraction of the price you pay at the boutiques. Temptation prevails right up until leaving the country – Brussels International Airport is the biggest chocolate selling point in the world.

Entertainment

An opera performance sparked the revolution for Belgian independence, so it's not surprising the performing arts are celebrated across the country. Brussels boasts dozens of superb venues, while Bruges has its own state-of-the-art venue, Concertgebouw. There are also charming traditional puppet theatres, notably the Théâtre Royal de Toone.

Belgian Cinema

The Belgian love of cinema seems easily explained by two things: the fact that nightlife doesn't start until late, and the climate. The country brims with cinemas, though the industry itself is underfunded compared with other art forms. An average of just two mainstream Belgian films are released per year, in addition to smaller, lower-budget independent releases. But Belgian directors are internationally renowned, chief among them brothers Luc and Jean-Pierre Dardenne. Their film *The Kid with a Bike* won the Grand Prix at Cannes Film Festival in 2011, while harrowing *Rosetta* (1999) and the rather more uplifting *L'Enfant* (2005) were both awarded the Palme d'Or. Bruges itself also starred memorably in 2008's hilarious action-comedy *In Bruges,* in which Colin Farrell and Brendan Gleeson play hitmen ordered by their boss (Ralph Fiennes) to hide out in the city during the pre-Christmas frenzy.

Local Stars

Unlike its directors, Belgium's film stars generally aren't well known outside their own country, the exception being Brussels' action-hero Jean-Claude Van Damme. Other local stars include Vincent Grass, Natacha Amal and Matthias Schoenaerts.

Best Theatre, Music & Dance in Bruges

Koninklijke Stadsschouwburg A grand venue for classical music, dance and theatre. (p51)

Concertgebouw (pictured) This modern concert hall

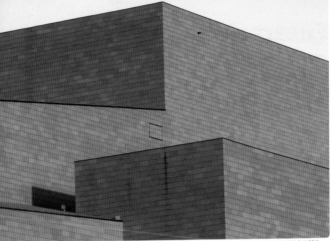

JONATHAN SMITH/LONELY PLANET ©

shows top-drawer music and dance. (p72)

Cactus Muziekcentrum World and modern music, with its own music festival. (p73)

Best Theatre, Music & Dance in Brussels

BOZAR A big-hitter venue that hosts major orchestras. (p120)

Art Base Chamber music is on the varied program at this small venue. (p97)

Théâtre Royal de Toone Eight generations of Toone family puppetry; a highlight of any visit to Brussels. (p97)

Best Cinemas

Cinéma Galeries Art-house flicks in a 19th-century gallery. (Brussels; p96)

Palace Cinema The city's oldest cinema, renewed and restored. (Brussels; p98)

Cinematek Daily silent movies with live piano accompaniment. (Brussels; p120)

Cinema Lumière Art-house cinema screening foreign films in their original language. (Bruges; p51)

Film Houses vs Cinemas

There's no need to seek out cinema chains in the capital: the most characterful film houses are small and independent, tucked away in elegant glassed galleries and down side streets.

Festivals & Events

Not even the notoriously fickle climate can rain on Belgium's parade when it's time to party. Brussels and Bruges each host a slew of diverse events, especially midyear. And the short distances between the cities means you're only a train ride away from some sort of festivity.

Party All Night

One of the annual highlights in Brussels is the Nuit Blanche (White Night; www. brusselsinter national.be) in September. The idea is borrowed from Paris and has spread globally: for one 'white night', the capital stays up until sunrise, laying on a swath of events, including projections, instal-lations, circus acts and parties, blues and more in Brussels' Jardin Botanique.

Procession of the Holy Blood

This large Catholic procession of the 'Holy Blood' in Bruges dates back to the Middle Ages. At the heart of the procession is a cloth reputedly stained with the blood of Jesus, brought to Flanders in the 12th century. It takes place each Ascension Day.

Information

In addition to the tour-ist offices' websites, a good place to find out what's on is *Agenda* (www.brusselsagen da.be), a lively events

magazine published weekly in English, French and Dutch. Many festival dates vary from year to year; check the websites for details.

Best Music Festivals

Ars Musica (www.arsmu sica.be; Brussels; ⊙Mar) Audiences get wired into the contemporary music scene at this accessible festival.

Les Nuits Botanique (www. botanique.be; Brussels; ⊙May) Twelve days of rock, reggae, ska, hip hop, electro, folk, rap, blues and more in Jardin Botanique.

Couleur Café Festival (www.couleurcafe.be; Brus-sels; ⊙late Jun) Performers

ALEXANDROS MICHAILIDIS/SHUTTERSTOCK ©

at this three-day world-music and dance knees-up have included James Brown and UB40.

Musica Antiqua (www.mafestival.be; Bruges; ☉Aug) This festival of early music not only includes concerts but hands-on workshops such as harpsichord maintenance.

Best Food & Drink Festivals

Brussels Food Truck Festival (www.brusselsfoodtruckfestival.com; Brussels; ☉May) Lovers of street-food converge on the Boulevard de l'Impératrice and Mont des Arts for one of the world's largest food-truck festivals.

Belgian Beer Weekend (www.belgianbrewers.be; Brussels; ☉Sep) The Grand Place is overtaken by a veritable village of stalls selling beer and associated paraphernalia (glasses, coasters etc.). Drink prices are reasonable and entry is free.

Best of the Rest

Ommegang (www.ommegang.be; Brussels; ☉Jul) Dating from the 14th century, this medieval-style procession (pictured) kicks off from the Place du Grand Sablon, ending with a dance in the illuminated Grand Place.

Brussels Summer Festival (www.bsf.be; Brussels; ☉Aug) Free 10-day bash packing in more than 140 different performances (concerts, children's theatre and more), including many local acts.

Comic Strip Festival (www.fetedelabd.be; Brussels; ☉Sep) Rub shoulders with the artists and writers behind some of Belgium's best-known comic characters.

Museums & Galleries

Bruges and Brussels have a rich artistic tradition stretching back centuries; in true Belgian style, you'll also find irreverent sculptures and comic murals on display. The art movement that really captured Belgium was surrealism, and leading the charge was René Magritte, whose man in a bowler hat has become a national emblem.

Belgian Art

The distinction between Dutch and Flemish painters didn't come about until the late-16th century. However, the artists who were commissioned in the 15th century by nobility to record their life, times and religion, and would go on to influence the direction of European art, are today known as the Flemish Primitives. The 16th century saw Flemish painter Pieter Brueghel the Elder and his two sons, Pieter the Younger and Jan, make their mark on the artistic landscape. Perhaps Belgium's most renowned painter, though, was Pieter Paul Rubens (1577–1640). Born in Germany, Rubens returned to his parents' home town of Antwerp and utilised both Flemish and Italian styles to create his seminal religious works and voluptuous 'Rubenesque' nudes.

Contemporary Art

Belgium has a powerful contemporary art scene. Look out for works by Panamarenko, whose bizarre sculptures and paintings fuse authentic and imaginary flying contraptions; Jan Fabre, famed for his Bic-art (ballpoint pen drawings); powerful politically themed paintings by Luc Tuymans; and Eddy Stevens, who combines elements of Rubens' lustrous realism with surrealist twists.

RADIOKAFKA/SHUTTERSTOCK ©

Best Flemish Primitives

Musées Royaux des Beaux-Arts (pictured) A wonderful showcase of the work of Van der Weyden and co. (Brussels; p108)

Groeningemuseum Sublime works by the masters of refined oil-painting. (Bruges; p56)

Museum Sint-Janshospitaal Six jewel-bright works by the great Hans Memling. (Bruges; p58)

Best Speciality Museums, Bruges

Historium An immersive audio-visual and virtual-reality trip through time. (p37)

Volkskundemuseum An appealing folk museum in an old *godshuis* (almshouse). (p44)

Choco-Story All you ever wanted to know about chocolate. (p45)

Frietmuseum Only in Belgium: a celebration of the humble French fry. (p45)

Best Speciality Museums, Brussels

Musée des Sciences Naturelles Belgium's national museum of Natural Sciences. (p131)

Musée Magritte Surrealist fun: paintings, films, photos and sketches. (p109)

Musée BELvue Take a trip through Belgian history. (p116)

Musée Art & Histoire Royal museum of art nouveau and art deco treasures. (p128)

Architecture

Bruges and Brussels both present a compelling cross-section of building styles – the fabulous architecture is the reason many visitors are here. Contemporary architecture has lagged behind, but a few ground-breaking buildings are rising on the skyline, such as Bruges' red-brick concert hall, the Concertgebouw.

JEAN-BERNARD CARILLET/LONELY PLANET ©

Tours

Get up close and personal with Brussels' architecture with the resident-run heritage conservation group, **ARAU** (Atelier de Recherche et d'Action Urbaines; ☎ 02-219 33 45; www.arau.org; Blvd Adolphe Max 55; tours €10-20; ⏰ Apr–mid-Dec; Ⓜ De Brouckère).

Best Art Nouveau Architecture

Old England Building Gorgeous former department store, now home to MIM. (Brussels; p110)

Centre Belge de la Bande Dessinée Housed in a gorgeous Horta building. (Brussels; p82)

Maison Cauchie (pictured) Art nouveau glamour in the EU district. (Brussels; p127)

Best Churches

Église Notre-Dame du Sablon Medieval gem on a lovely square. (Brussels; p114)

Cathédrale des Sts-Michel & Gudule Grand cathedral in the style of Paris' Notre Dame. (Brussels; p86)

Jeruzalemkerk Dramatically modelled on the Church of the Holy Sepulchre in Jerusalem. (Bruges; p44)

Onze-Lieve-Vrouwekerk Huge 13th-century church with a Michelangelo statue. (Bruges; p66)

Best of the Rest

Belfort Massive, awe-inspiring belfry. (Bruges; p37)

Grand Place Ringed by splendid, gabled guildhalls. (Brussels; p80)

Galeries St-Hubert Glamorous glass-covered shopping arcade. (Brussels; p86)

Palais de Justice Monumental, brooding law courts. (Brussels; p117)

Berlaymont Building Star-shaped building housing EU commissioners. (Brussels; p133)

LGBT+ Life

STANISLAVBELOGLAZOV/SHUTTERSTOCK ©

Brussels is Belgium's magnet for LGBT+ visitors. In general, the attitude to gay visitors is relaxed and accepting. In terms of legislation, Belgium is progressive about rights for same-sex couples.

Events

The legendary event is the city's monthly La Démence club night, held at Fuse, when bold and beautiful boys from all over Europe come to kick up their heels. The Festival du Film Gay & Lesbien de Bruxelles (p147) takes place in late January, while the Belgian Gay & Lesbian Pride (p147) parade hits the streets in May.

The Scene

Brussels' gay and lesbian scene is concentrated around the compact but thriving Rainbow Quarter, centred around Rue du Marché au Charbon, Rue des Pierres and Rue de la Fourche in the heart of the city. Bruges' scene is more subdued. The tourist office keeps an updated list of gay-friendly establishments. An excellent website for all things LGBT+ in Belgium is www.lumi.be, which, although in Dutch, is fairly easy to navigate and lists dozens of venues throughout the country. Also try www.gayscout.com and www.travelgay.com for listings.

Best LGBT+ friendly venues in Brussels

Chez Maman Features the capital's most beloved drag show. (p98)

Le Belgica DJs transform what looks like a 1920s traditional brown cafe into one of Brussels' most popular gay music pubs. (p96)

Fuse Once a month it hosts epic gay night La Démence. (p119)

Cabaret Mademoiselle Brussels' sauciest new burlesque-themed venue. (p97)

Markets

The full spectrum of markets is set up regularly in Bruges and Brussels – from elegant antiques markets and fairs trading rare china, crystal and furniture to flea markets spilling over with bric-a-brac), secondhand treasures and clothing. There are also rainbow-like food markets, where you can pick up the ingredients for the perfect picnic.

CHRISTIAN MUELLER/SHUTTERSTOCK ©

Market Nosh

Any time of year, the street fare sold from caravans parked at the markets is a treat: try steaming waffles that tickle your nose with icing sugar and cones full of mayonnaise-slathered fries.

Christmas Markets

Christmas season brings the most magical markets of all, when the cities' ancient squares fill with stalls selling handcrafted toys, nutcrackers, a dazzling array of ornaments and warming mugs of sweet mulled wine. Winter wonderlands of ice sculptures and outdoor skating rinks are erected most years. Both generally take place throughout the month of December. Tourist offices can advise as to the markets' venues, but you can't go wrong just following the crowds.

Best Markets

Markt Historic Wednesday market ringed by stunning architecture (Bruges; p36)

Place du Jeu-de-Balle Flea Market Sharpen your elbows for the daily giveaway of unsold stock. (Brussels; p121)

Sablon Antiques Market Mosey around for treasures at this weekend market. (Brussels; p121)

Grand Place Hosts a flower market three times a week on Monday, Wednesday and Friday mornings. (Brussels; p80)

Place Jourdan Market Sunday market for food and clothes in EU Quarter. (Brussels; p137)

PYTY/SHUTTERSTOCK ©

Parks & Gardens

The cities' parks and gardens offer more than a breath of fresh air; they're also oases of art, history and culture. The big smoke, Brussels, is greener than you might expect, with parks right in the heart of the city plus forest on the outer fringes. Bruges has some beautiful parks lining its waterways, including one dotted with working windmills.

Brussels Parks

The most popular of Brussels' parks – attracting everyone from lunching office workers to joggers and pram-pushing parents – is the Parc de Bruxelles. In the shadow of the Palais Royal and the Palais de la Nation, this gracious former hunting ground was laid out in the 18th century, and was the scene of bloody fighting in 1830 during Belgium's bid for independence.

In the EU quarter, the vast Parc du Cinquantenaire is ringed by museums. At the city's southeastern edge, the wooded parkland of the Bois de la Cambre sprawls to meet the forest of the Forêt de Soignes, while in the city's northwest, the chestnut- and magnolia-shaded Parc de Laeken extends to the Atomium.

Best Green Spaces

Parc du Cinquantenaire Park surrounded by Brussels' top museums. (Brussels; p126)

Parc Léopold Take a leafy break in the heart of the EU area. (Brussels; p132)

Parc de Bruxelles One of the capital's prettiest parks. (Brussels; p114)

Minnewater (pictured) Secluded paths wind around the 'Lake of Love'. (Bruges; p61)

Begijnhof The peaceful courtyard of Begijnhof is dotted with daffodils in spring. (Bruges; p60)

For Kids

The exquisite chocolate boutiques and treasure trove of museums might be aimed squarely at adults, but little visitors will also get a kick out of visiting these two cities. Although Bruges doesn't have a huge range of child-specific museums, the entire city is like one great big fairytale castle when viewed through the eyes of a child.

ISHAN NAMAN SINHA/SHUTTERSTOCK ©

Travel Practicalities

Many B&Bs and hotels have baby cribs. Reserve these as places often have just one on hand. Think twice about bringing a stroller, as you'll be wrestling it up and down endless flights of stairs and negotiating narrow footpaths and cobblestones. Dining with kids is rarely a problem, even at top-end establishments. You'll rarely see Belgian kids running amok, and you will be expected to make sure yours aren't either. Restaurants often have high chairs, and sometimes special children's menus, but it's worth confirming in advance. With waffles and fries proliferating throughout both cities, you may be in for a bit of arm-twisting, but kids won't go hungry.

Best for Kids in Bruges

Historium This museum's exciting VR exhibits will kick-start your kids' interest in history. (p37)

Choco-Story The only downside to this delicious museum is the crash after the sugar high. (p45)

Frietmuseum Visit this celebration of French fries around lunchtime for best effect. (p45)

Bruges Canal Tours Adults and kids ooh and aah on magical tours of medieval waterways. (p27)

Best for Kids in Brussels

Centre Belge de la Bande Dessinée A temple to all things Tintin in a gorgeous art nouveau building. (p82)

Musée des Sciences Naturelles (pictured) Walk with the dinosaurs at this striking museum. (p131)

Théâtre Royal de Toone Fabulous and traditional puppet theatre in a medieval building. (p97)

Tours

S-F/SHUTTERSTOCK ©

Best Bus & Boat Tours

Bruges Canal Tours

(Bruges; Map p64, E1; adult/child €8/4; ⏱10am-6pm Mar–mid-Nov) The must-do activity is to see the city by water on a 30-minute canal boat tour. Boats depart roughly every 20 minutes from jetties south of Markt and Burg.

Legends Walking Tours

(Bruges; ☎0472 26 87 15; www.legendstours.be/walking-tours-bruges; Markt; admission free) This highly lauded operator runs a series of wildly popular free walking tours which are a great way to get oriented before making your own explorations of the city.

Lamme Goedzak

(Bruges; ☎050-28 86 10; www.bootdamme-brugge.be; Noorweegse Kaai 31; adult/child one-way €8.50/6, return €10.50/9.50; ⏱10am-5pm Easter–mid-Oct) The Lamme Goedzak tourist

paddle steamer chugs its way on 35-minute boat trips to the enchanting town of Damme, with two or three sailings per day.

Quasimodo

(Bruges; ☎050-37 04 70; www.quasimodo.be; Veldmaarschalk Fochstraat 69; under/over 26yr €55/65) Quasimodo runs minibus Triple Treat tours, visiting a selection of castles and the fascinating WWII coastal defences near Ostend.

Brussels by Water

(Brussels; ☎02-201 10 50; www.brusselsbywater.be; Quai des Péniches 2b; trips from €10; Ⓜ Ribaucourt) Brussels' canals offer an interesting (if industrial) perspective of the capital.

Brussels City Tours

(Brussels; ☎02-513 77 44; www.brussels-city-tours.com; Rue du Marché aux Herbes; adult/concession/child €29/26/15; ⏱10am; Ⓜ Gare Centrale) These three-hour tours cover everything from the Ato-

mium to the EU, and include some lovely art nouveau houses.

Best Bicycle Tours

Quasimundo

(Bruges; ☎050-33 07 75; www.quasimundo.eu; Predikherenstraat 28; adult/student €28/26; ⏱Mar-Oct) Guided bicycle tours around town (2½ hours, morning) or via Damme to the Dutch border (four hours, afternoons). Bike rental is included. Book ahead.

Groovy Brussels Bike Tours

(Brussels; ☎0484 89 89 36; www.groovybrussels.com/brussels-bike-tour; tour incl bicycle rental €29; ⏱10am daily Apr-Oct, plus 2pm Sat & Sun; Ⓜ Gare Centrale) Many first-time visitors to Brussels love this tour for the ride and for the beer and *frites* stops along the way (at own expense). Chocolate- and beer-themed tours are also available.

Perfect Days

Day 1 – Bruges

PECOLD/SHUTTERSTOCK ©

Stroll past the **fish market** (p53) along the famous canals or take a half-hour **canal cruise** (p66). Climb the **Belfort** (p37) for bird's-eye views, then descend to see Bruges' holiest relic in the **Basiliek van het Heilig Bloed** (pictured, p39). Lunch with the locals at **De Belegde Boterham** (p41) before admiring Belgian art at the **Groeningemuseum** (p56) and taking a stroll around the serene **begijnhof** (p60), being sure to visit the little house museum there. Tour **Brouwerij De Halve Maan** (p66), where Brugse Zot is made. Dine at **Den Dyver** (p69), where beer is paired with each dish and used in its preparation, then finish your day at the city's oldest pub, the picturesque **Herberg Vlissinghe** (p48).

Day 2 – Bruges

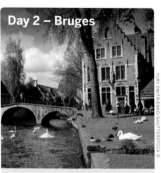

YURY DMITRIENKO/SHUTTERSTOCK ©

Take a morning wander around the St-Anna district, visiting the **Jeruzalemkerk** (p44), and the **Volkskundemuseum** (p44). Stop for a pub lunch and a *gueuze* (lambic beer) at **De Windmolen** (p49) from where you can gaze upon one of the city's working windmills, before pressing on to take in the art and architecture of **Museum Sint-Janshospitaal** (p58) and its world-renowned Memling paintings. Wander through **Minnewater Park** (pictured, p61) to delightful **De Stoepa** (p69) for an aperitif in its agreeable courtyard, then dine at lively **L'Estaminet** (p71; book ahead) and take in a show at **Concertgebouw** (p72). Round out your evening with a romantic gas-lamp-lit stroll to **De Republiek** (p50) for a nightcap.

Day 3 – Brussels

Brussels' splendid **Grand Place** (p80) is the perfect spot to kick off a tour of the capital. While here, pop into the **Brussels City Museum** (p87), then stroll through the glass-roofed **Galeries St-Hubert** (pictured, p86) to **Cathédrale des Sts-Michel & Gudule** (p86). Head to **MIM** (p110) in Mont des Arts for lunch at its rooftop cafe and allow at least two hours to tour the museum. Take an afternoon stroll in the spacious **Parc de Bruxelles** (p114) opposite, then head downhill for dinner and jazz at **Le Cercle des Voyageurs** (p91). Alternatively, take the glass lift outside the colossal **Palais de Justice** (p117) to the Marolles area to dine at one of its renowned restaurants – try **L'Idiot du Village** (p117).

Day 4 – Brussels

Browse boutiques along Rue Antoine Dansaert, then head to the costume and lace museum, **Musée Mode & Dentelle** (p86). Take the metro to visit **Musée Art & Histoire** (p128), with rich collections of antiquities, the **House of European History** (p132), or the **Musée des Sciences Naturelles** (p131) or find out about the workings of the EU at **Parlamentarium** (pictured, p132). Stroll around leafy **Parc du Cinquantenaire** (p126). Start the evening at **Le Cirio** (p94) before seeing a traditional puppet show at the quaint **Théâtre Royal de Toone** (p97), or enjoy some live music and dining at the **Music Village** (p96), **BOZAR** (p120) or **L'Archiduc** (p96) before returning to **Grand Place** (p80) to marvel at the dazzling lighting.

Need to Know

For detailed information, see Survival Guide (p141)

Currency
euro (€)

Languages Spoken
Dutch in Bruges; Dutch and French in Brussels

Visas
EU citizens can stay indefinitely; many other nationals can enter visa-free for up to 90 days.

Money
Credit cards are widely accepted. ATMs are very prevalent.

Mobile Phones
Non-EU visitors are best off buying a local SIM card for their GSM phone.

Time
Central European Time (GMT/UTC plus one hour)

Tipping
Tipping is not required in restaurants, bars or taxis.

Daily Budget

Budget: Less than €100

Dorm bed including breakfast: €22–30

Midweek lunch: €10–15

Train ticket: €10

Museum entry: €5–15

Beer: €2–4

Short-hop city bike hire: €2

Midrange: €100–250

Double room at B&B or midrange hotel: €60–140

Two-course meal with wine for two: €80–110

Top end: More than €250

Double room at better hotel or top B&B: €140–200

Cocktails: €9–20

Degustation meal with wine for two: €180–350

Advance Planning

Three months before Travel is much more affordable if booked in advance, particularly if you're travelling by train.

One month before Book Bruges accommodation early, particularly in high season.

Two weeks before Book a Brussels Greeters (p115) for insider insight. Make reservations for top-flight restaurants.

One week before Make a wish list of things to see and do – you're bound to be distracted once you arrive.

A few days before Buy concert and theatre tickets online.

Arriving in Bruges & Brussels

✈ Brussels Airport

A smooth system of trains and buses greets you at Brussels Airport; the quickest option is the Airport City Express train (to Bruxelles-Central €10, 20 minutes).

✈ Charleroi Airport

Coaches wait right outside the terminal to take visitors into the centre (€14.20/28.40 one way/return; 1½ hours).

🚉 Bruxelles-Central

Eurostar, TGV and Thalys high-speed trains arrivehere, from where you can walk or take the metro to your destination.

🚉 Bruxelles-Nord

Eurolines buses arrive at Bruxelles-Nord, linked by metro to the rest of the city.

🚉 Bruges Central Station

Located 1.5km south of Markt. Intercity and international bus services use the bus interchange adjacent the station.

Getting Around

🚗 Car & Motorcycle

Best avoided in both cities.

᪣ Bicycle

Brussels boasts a network of bike lanes and separate bike paths. Bruges is less bike-friendly.

🚉 Public transport

Brussels' bus-tram-metro system is operated by STIB/MIVB (p144). It runs from about 6am to midnight. Bruges city buses are operated by DeLijn (p144) and run from 5.30am to 11pm.

Taxi

Official taxis run meters and have standard fares.

PORNPOJ/SHUTTERSTOCK ©

Bruges Neighbourhoods

Markt, Burg & North Bruges (p35)
Two stunning, interlinked squares are the perfect introduction to the medieval city, and the surrounding lanes are delightful for exploring.

Markt

Burg

Groeningemuseum

Museum Sint-Janshospitaal

Begijnhof

South Bruges (p55)
Bruges' major museums are here, including standout collections of the Flemish Primitives, while the Begijnhof is a green retreat.

Explore Bruges

If you set out to design a fairy-tale medieval town, it would be hard to improve on central Bruges (Brugge in Dutch), one of Europe's best preserved cities. Picturesque cobbled lanes and dreamy canals link photogenic market squares lined with soaring towers, historical churches and lane after lane of old whitewashed almshouses.

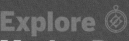

Explore

Markt, Burg & North Bruges

Encircled by a canal that loops around the old town, the geographical and spiritual heart of Bruges centres on the adjacent Markt and Burg areas, linked by Breidelstraat. Here you'll find the mainstay of the city's medieval sights. Locals refer to the 'north' as the area including Markt, Burg and all points north within the loop.

The heart of Bruges is centred around its spacious Markt (p36), with its soaring Belfort (p37) and beautiful medieval architecture. The modern Historium (p37) museum is an easy first port-of-call. Burg (p38), an adjacent, smaller square, is Bruges' centuries-old administrative hub. Be sure to explore the eye-catching Brugse Vrije (p39) and Stadhuis (p39), inside which you'll find the astonishing Gotische Zaal (p39), a hall elaborately decorated like no other. Much of Bruges' magic is uncovered by losing yourself in this area's warren of little lanes, picturesque canals and postcard-perfect streetscapes, at their most magnificent after dark, when the cobblestones and canals are romantically illuminated by gas lamps and moonlight.

Getting There & Around

🚌 Any bus marked Centrum will take you into Markt from Bruges' bus station.

🏃 Alternatively, by foot, follow the crowds on the well-signposted route along Oostmeers (1.5km).

Neighbourhood Map on p42

View towards Markt (p36) OLENA Z/SHUTTERSTOCK ©

Top Sight 📷
Markt

*Flanked by medieval-style step-gabled build-ings, this splendid open market square is Bruges'
nerve centre, lined with pavement cafés beneath
step-gabled facades. Horse-drawn carriages clatter between open-air restaurants and camera-
clicking tourists, all watched over by Bruges'
spectacular Belfort and a verdigris-green statue
of Pieter De Coninck and Jan Breydel, the leaders
of the Bruges Matins revolt.*

◉ MAP P42, C4

Belfort

The symbol of Bruges is its Unesco-listed, 13th-century **belfry** (Belfort; ☎ 050-44 87 43; www.visitbruges.be/nl/belfort; Markt 7; adult/child €12/10; ⊙ 9.30am-6pm), rising a lofty 83m above Markt. Ascending the 366 steps brings you past the treasury, a triumphal bell and a 47-bell, manually operated carillon, which still regularly chimes across the city. Once at the top, look out across the spires and red-tiled rooftops towards the wind turbines and giant cranes of Zeebrugge.

Historium

The **Historium** (☎ 050-27 03 11; www.historium. be; Markt; adult/child €14/7.50; ⊙ 10am-6pm) occupies a fine neo-Gothic building on the northern side of the square. Taking visitors back to 1435, it is an immersive multimedia experience, claiming to be more a medieval movie than a museum: you can survey the old port or watch Van Eyck paint. It's a little light on facts, so for many it will be a diversion from the real sights of the city.

Market

Appropriately enough, this historical market square is still the location for a major food market held on Wednesday mornings. Locals and tourist mix to purchase cheeses, sausages, spit-roasted meat, fruit, vegetables and plants. Authentic waffles are sold from a van, and the Belfort looms picturesquely over the proceedings.

Eiermarkt

Immediately to the north and adjoining Markt, this little square can be identified by a stone column surmounted by lions. It's ringed by *cafés* and bars, and is a marginally cheaper and less frenetic place for a coffee or a drink than Markt itself.

★ Top Tips

○ If you're visiting lots of sights, consider buying a Musea Brugge Card (p146).

○ Be sure to visit the square at night, when it's quieter and beautifully lit.

○ Carriage tours (€50 for up to five people) depart from Markt and take 30 minutes, including a pit stop at the *begijn-hof* (p60).

○ In summer, aim to make a carriage trip between 6pm and 7pm when the buildings glow golden in the sun's late rays.

✗ Take a Break

For coffee, cake or bagels, head halfway down Sint-Amandsstraat to the **Gingerbread Tea Room** (Map p42, B4; ☎ 0494 52 19 78; Sint-Amandsstraat 29; breakfast €10-13; ⊙ 9am-5pm).

If it's the contrast of upscale dining in a modern setting you seek, it's a short stroll east to Lieven (p46).

Top Sight 📷

Burg

Just east of Markt, the less theatrical but still enchanting Burg has been Bruges' administrative centre for centuries. It's common to find public art installations in the square that contrast the modern with the medieval. Burg's southern flank incorporates three superb interlinked facades that glow with gilded detail. The city's Stadhuis and Brugse Vrije dominate the square.

◎ MAP P42, D4

Brugse Vrije

This wonderful, eye-catching **building** ([☎]050-44 87 11; Burg 11a; €6; [⏱]9.30am-noon & 1.30-5pm), with early baroque gables and golden statuettes, was once the seat of the 'Liberty of Bruges', the large autonomous territory that was ruled from Bruges between 1121 and 1794. The building still houses city offices, but you can visit the Renaissancezaal to admire its remarkable 1531 carved chimney piece. To reach a photogenic spot by the canal, wander along pretty Blinde Ezelstraat between the Brugse Vrije and the Stadhuis.

Stadhuis

The beautiful 1420 **Stadhuis** (City Hall; [☎]050-44 87 43; www.visitbruges.be/en/stadhuis-city-hall; Burg 12; adult/concession/under 18yr €6/5/free; [⏱]9.30am-5pm) has a fanciful facade covered with replica statues of the counts and countesses of Flanders (the originals were torn down in 1792 by French soldiers). Inside, an audioguide explains numerous portraits before leading you upstairs to the astonishing **Gotische Zaal** (Gothic Hall; pictured). Few rooms anywhere achieve such a jaw-dropping first impression as this dazzling hall with its polychrome ceiling, hanging vaults and romantic historical murals.

Basiliek van het Heilig Bloed

The western end of the stadhuis morphs into the **Basiliek van het Heilig Bloed** (Basilica of the Holy Blood; [☎]050-33 67 92; www.holyblood.com; Burg 13; €2; [⏱]9.30am-noon & 2-5pm, closed Wed afternoons mid-Nov–Mar), which takes its name from a phial supposedly containing a few drops of Christ's blood that was brought here after the 12th-century Crusades. The right-hand door leads upstairs to a colourful chapel where the relic is hidden behind a flamboyant silver tabernacle.

★ Top Tips

The Holy Blood relic in the basilica is brought out for veneration at 2pm daily – respectful and quiet visitors are welcome.

Burg is at its most tranquil and beautiful in the early evening and at night.

South of Burg and across the bridge, the lovely 1821 Vismarkt (p53) still accommodates fish stalls most mornings, along with trinket sellers later in the day.

✗ Take a Break

Try tiny De Garre (p48) for local brews with a local crew, tucked away on an alley between Markt and Burg.

For a light lunch with a waterside setting, nab a table at Opus Latino (p47).

Walking Tour 🥾

Shop Local in Central Bruges

Central Bruges can sometimes feel like a melee of waffle stands and frites stalls. But it's worth remembering that this is indeed a real place, where discerning locals do their shopping, eating and drinking. There are some real finds if you're looking for interesting beers, cheeses and charcuterie, as well as fashion, lace and bric-a-brac.

Walk Facts

Start Markt
End L'Estaminet
Length 2.3km

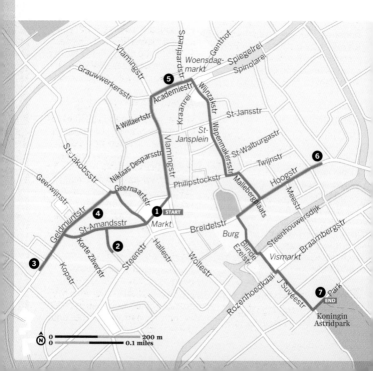

❶ Markt

Markt (p36) is tourist central, crammed with horse carriages and tour groups. But come on Wednesday mornings for a genuinely local, excellent food market. Speciality cheeses, sausages, picnic fare and fresh fruit are among the offerings.

❷ De Belegde Boterham

Duck the tourist crowds at this popular lunch **spot** (☎050-34 91 31; www.debelegdeboterham.be; Kleine St-Amandsstraat 5; mains €14-22; ☺noon-4pm Mon-Sat) for well-heeled locals. The monochrome boutique styling is a bit formal, but it's a friendly place and the food – soups, sandwiches and large salads – is excellent, with fresh ingredients and tasty dressings. Good coffee too.

❸ L'Heroine

L'Heroine (☎050-33 56 57; www. lheroine.be; Noordzandstraat 32; ☺10.30am-6pm Mon-Sat) features established Belgian designers Dries Van Noten and Ann Demeulemeester, plus young talents such as Christian Wijnants. It stocks beautiful silk print dresses, asymmetrical tailoring and sumptuous scarves and drapes – staff can help you combine pieces for a strong, idiosyncratic look.

❹ Diksmuids Boterhuis

This gorgeous traditional **grocery** (www.diksmuidsboterhuis.be; Geldmuntstraat 23; ☺10am-12.30pm & 2-6.30pm) has been here since 1933. Decked out with red-and-white gingham flounces and featuring a ceiling hung with sausages, it sells cheeses, honey, cold meats and mustard.

❺ Bacchus Cornelius

When locals want a special tipple, they come to **Bacchus Cornelius** (☎050-34 53 38; www.bacchus cornelius.com; Academiestraat 17; ☺1-6.30pm). There are 450 beers and rare *gueuzes* (type of lambic beer), as well as *jenevers* (gins) and liqueurs flavoured with elderflower, cranberries and cherries. Ask the shop owner if you can try her home-brewed, silky smooth *jenever*, made with real chocolate.

❻ Madam Mim

This adorable **shop** (☎050-61 55 05; www.madammim.be; Hoogstraat 29; ☺11am-6pm Wed-Mon) sells quirky clothes handmade from vintage fabrics by shop owner Mim, as well as '60s crockery, cut glass, glorious hats and '70s kids' clothes. You can also pick up antique lace for a fraction of the price it goes for elsewhere.

❼ L'Estaminet

With its weighty dark-timber beams and low lighting, L'Estaminet (p71) barely seems to have changed since it opened in 1900. In summer, patrons spill out onto the terrace.

Bruges Markt, Burg & North Bruges

N

0   200 m
0   0.1 miles

For reviews see
- Top Sights   p36
- Sights   p44
- Eating   p46
- Drinking   p48
- Entertainment   p51
- Shopping   p52

Gouden Handrei

St-Jorisstr
Augustijnenrei
Kortewinkel
Vlamingstr
Kipstr
Spanjaardstr

Woensdag-markt

Grauwwerkersstr

Ezelstr
Oude Zak
Rozendal

12 St-Jakobs-plein

Academiestr

6 Frietmuseum

Lumina Domestica; Choco-Story 4

Naaldenstr
Kuipersstr

A Willaertstr
Kraanplein
27
St-Jansstr
J Van Ooststr

Winzakstr
Wapenmakersstr

Boterhuis

24
30
St-Jakobsstr
29

9
Niklaas Desparsstr

Cordoeaniersstr
22
7

Philipstockstr

St-Jakobs-plein

Leeuwstr
Geerwijnstr
Palmstr

Eiermarkt

Markt (Historium) InfoKantoor

Muntplein
Moerstr

23
Geldmuntstr
Muntpoort
17
13
St-Amandsstr

Beer Experience
3 Breidelstr

Markt

Burg

Ontvangersstr
Kopstr

Gingerbread Tea Room
Kleine St-Amandsstr
8

32

Belfort
33
Halestr

19 Stadhuis
15

Korte Zilverstr

St-Niklaasstr

Wollestr
Kartuizerinnenstr
35

Helmstr
Haanstr
Noordzandstr
Giststr
Zilverstr
Kemelstr

Loppemstr

Simon Stevinplein

Oude Burg
Nieuwstr

Canal Cruises

Wulfhagestr

26

31

Steenstr

Dijver

Noordzandstr
10

Canal Cruises

Het Zand
11
37
Dweerstr
Zuidzandstr
Lendestr

Mariastr

Heilige Geeststr
Korte Vuldersstr

Goezeputstr

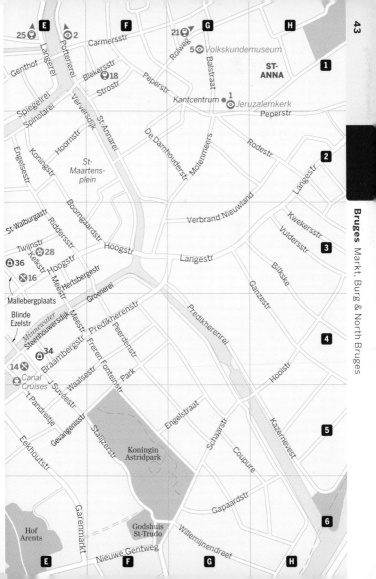

Sights

Jeruzalemkerk   CHURCH

1 ⊚ MAP P42, G1

Within the so-caled **Adornes-domein** estate is one of Bruges' oddest churches, the 15th-century Jeruzalemkerk, built by the Adornes family. Supposedly based on Jerusalem's Church of the Holy Sepulchre, it's a macabre monument with a gruesome altarpiece covered in skull motifs and an effigy of Christ's corpse tucked away in the rear mini-chapel. The entry price includes admission to a small museum occupying several of the estate's pretty almshouses. (📞050-33 88 83; www.adornes.org/en; Peperstraat 3; adult/concession €7/3.50; ⊙church & museum 10am-5pm Mon-Sat)

OLV-ter-Potterie   MUSEUM

2 ⊚ MAP P42, E1

Admission to this small historical church-hospital complex is free with a Sint-Janshospitaal (p58) museum ticket. Ring the bell to gain entry and you'll find fine 15th-to 16th-century art. The lushly baroque church section houses the reliquary of St-Idesbaldus and a polychrome wooden relief of Mary breastfeeding baby Jesus. In later, more prudish centuries, the Virgin's nipple received a lacy camouflage, rendering the scene bizarrely impractical. (Our Lady of the Pottery; 📞050-44 87 43; www.visitbruges.be/en/onze-lieve-vrouw-ter-potterie-our-lady-of-the-pottery; Potterierei 79; adult/concession/under 18yr €6/5/free; ⊙9.30am-12.30pm & 1.30-5pm)

Beer Experience   MUSEUM

3 ⊚ MAP P42, D4

Markt's newest attraction will appeal to the many who love a Belgian beer. Guided by a multilingual iPad app, the museum takes you through the history of beer, the brewing process and the various different types of beers in Belgium and beyond. Three tastings are included, or you can opt out for a reduced admission. There is, of course, a gift shop. (📞050-69 92 29; www.brugesbeermuseum.com; Breidelstraat 3; with/without 3 tastings €12/8; ⊙10am-6pm)

Lumina Domestica   MUSEUM

4 ⊚ MAP P42, D2

The enlightening Domestic Lamp Museum has over 6500 artefacts relating to domestic lighting throughout history, making it the largest collection of its kind. It sheds light on the history of the humble lamp and illuminates one's awareness about the consumption and conservation of energy. (📞050-61 22 37; www.luminadomestica.be; Wijnzakstraat 2; adult/child €7/5; ⊙10am-5pm)

Volkskundemuseum   MUSEUM

5 ⊚ MAP P42, G1

This appealing Museum of Folk Life presents visitors with 18 themed tableaux illustrating Flemish life in times gone by – a 1930s sweets shop, a hatter's workshop, a traditional kitchen and more. The museum is a static affair, but it's in an attractive *godshuis* (almshouse), and the time-warp museum *café* **De Zwarte Kat** (light meals €7-12; ⊙11.45am-2pm) has a fine selection of beer. Temporary exhibits upstairs are often worth a look. Traditional lollies are made here on the first and third Thursday of the month. (Museum of Folk Life; 🕿050-44 87 43; www.visitbruges.be/en/volkskundemuseum-folklore-museum; Balstraat 43; adult/concession/under 18yr €6/5/free; ⊙9.30am-5pm Tue-Sun)

Choco-Story MUSEUM

This highly absorbing chocolate museum (see 4 Map p42, D2) traces the cocoa bean back to its role as an Aztec currency. Learn about choco history, watch a video on cocoa production and sample a praline that's made as you watch (last demonstration 4.45pm). Cheaper combination tickets with a variety of other museums are available: see the website for details. (🕿050-61 22 37; www.choco-story.be; Wijnzakstraat 2; adult/child €8/5; ⊙10am-5pm)

Frietmuseum MUSEUM

6 ◉ MAP P42, C2

Follows the history of the potato from ancient Inca grave sites to the Belgian fryer. The entry fee includes a discount token for the basement *frituur* (chip shop; 11am to 3pm) that immodestly claims to fry the world's ultimate chips. (🕿050-34 01 50; www.frietmuseum.be; Vlamingstraat 33; adult/

Choco-Story

Escape the crowds

Don't be afraid to escape the sometimes maddening crowds and venture further afield than Markt or Burg in any direction: you'll have no trouble finding things that pique your interest. Bruges is the kind of place where getting lost is half the fun, and finding your way back is half the fun again.

concession/child €7/6/5; ⏱10am-5pm, closed Christmas–mid-Jan)

Eating

Lieven BELGIAN €€

7 MAP P42, D3

You'll need to book ahead for a table at this extremely popular, excellent-value Belgian bistro. It works wonders with local ingredients, and is recognised by its peers from around the country. Simple food done well in a trendy but relaxed environment. (📞050-68 09 75; www.etenbijlieven. be; Philipstockstraat 45; mains €22-34; ⏱noon-10pm Tue-Sun)

De Stove INTERNATIONAL €€

8 MAP P42, C4

Having just 20 seats keeps this gem intimate. Fish caught daily is the house speciality, but the monthly changing menu also includes the likes of wild boar fillet on oyster mushrooms. Everything,

from the bread to the ice cream, is homemade. Despite perennially rave reviews, this calm one-room family restaurant remains friendly, reliable and inventive, without a hint of tourist-tweeness. (📞050-33 78 35; www.restaurantdestove.be; Kleine St-Amandsstraat 4; mains €19-36, menu with/without wine €69/51; ⏱7-9pm Fri-Tue, noon-1.30pm Sun)

Le Mystique INTERNATIONAL €€€

9 MAP P42, C3

Fine dining in an opulent setting. Le Mystique offers à la carte and Michelin-starred seasonal set menus (recommended) for lunch and dinner. Dress to impress. (📞050-44 44 45; www.lemystique. be; Niklaas Desparsstraat 11; 4-course menus with/without wine €115/79; ⏱6.30pm-9.30pm Tue-Sat)

That's Toast BREAKFAST €

10 MAP P42, A5

Bruges' best breakfast restaurant has already gained a following with locals and visitors for its all-day breakfasts including everything from eggs and waffles to tea and toast. (📞050-68 82 27; Dweersstraat 4; breakfast €6-18; ⏱8.30am-4pm Wed-Sun)

Gran Kaffee De Passage BISTRO €€

11 MAP P42, A6

A mix of regulars and travellers staying at the adjoining **hostel** (d/tr from €64/98; 📶) give this candlelit, alternative art deco—style bistro one of the best atmospheres in town. Its menu of hearty traditional dishes, such as *stoverij* (local meat in beer sauce), as well as filling tofu creations, is a bargain. (☎050-34 02 32; www. passagebruges.com; Dweersstraat 26-28; mains €10-18; ⏰5-11pm Tue-Thu & Sun, noon-11pm Fri & Sat)

De Bottelier   MEDITERRANEAN €€

12 ✗ MAP P42, B2

Decorated with hats and old clocks, this adorable little restaurant sits above a wine shop overlooking a delightful canal-side garden. Diners are predominantly local. Reservations are wise. (☎050-33 18 60; www.debottelier.com; St-Jakobsstraat 63; mains €15-23; ⏰noon-10pm Tue-Fri, from 7pm Sat)

Chagall   BELGIAN €€

13 ✗ MAP P42, B4

Checked olive banquettes, candles, an upright piano and shelves cluttered with knick-knacks make you feel like you're dining in a family home. Seafood, including several variations on eel, is Chagall's forte, but it also does daily meat specials and good deals on two- and three-course menus. (☎050-33 61 12; www.restaurantchagall.be; St-Amandsstraat 40; mains €20-29; ⏰noon-9pm Thu-Tue)

Den Gouden Karpel   SEAFOOD €

14 ✗ MAP P42, E4

Take away or eat in, this sleek little *café*/bar is a great location for a jumpingly fresh seafood lunch, right by the fish market (p53). Crab sandwiches, smoked salmon salads, shrimp croquettes and oysters are on the menu. (☎050-33 33 89; www.dengoudenkarpel. be; Vismarkt 9-11; dishes from €4; ⏰11am-6pm Tue-Sat)

Opus Latino   TAPAS €€

15 ✗ MAP P42, D4

Modernist *café* with weather-worn terrace tables right at the waterside, where a canal dead-ends beside a Buddha-head fountain. Access is via the easily missed shopping passage that links Wollestraat to Burg, emerging near the Basilica of the Holy Blood (p39). Serves tapas, pastas and pizzas, as well as more substantial fare. (☎050-33 97 46; Burg 15; tapas €5-12, pasta €11-18; ⏰11am-10pm)

't Gulden Vlies   BELGIAN €€

16 ✗ MAP P42, E3

Intimate late-night restaurant with old-fashioned decor and good-value Belgian cuisine. (☎050-33 47 09; www.tguldenvlies.be; Mallebergplaats 17; mains €14-28; ⏰7-11pm Wed-Sat)

Da Vinci   ICE CREAM €

17 ✗ MAP P42, B4

Not being able to choose from the 40 luscious flavours of freshly made ice cream at this *gelateria* is a good thing, as it means you'll be offered small spoonfuls of free samples to help you decide. (Of

The Bruges Matins Revolt

The precocious wealth and independent-mindedness of Bruges' medieval guildsmen created political tensions with their French overlords. In 1302, when guildsmen refused to pay a new round of taxes, the French sent in a 2000-strong army to garrison the town. Undeterred, Pieter De Coninck, dean of the Guild of Weavers, and Jan Breydel, dean of the Guild of Butchers, led a revolt that would go down in Flanders' history books as the 'Bruges Matins' (Brugse Metten). Early in the morning on 18 May, guildsmen crept into town and murdered anyone who could not correctly pronounce the hard-to-say Dutch phrase 'schild en vriend' (shield and friend). This revolt sparked a widespread Flemish rebellion. A short-term Flemish victory six weeks later at the Battle of the Golden Spurs near Kortrijk gave medieval Flanders a very short-lived moment of independence.

course, that might just make the decision harder.) (📞 050-33 36 50; www.davinci-brugge.be; Geldmunt-straat 34; scoop €1.50; ⏰ 11am-10pm)

Drinking

Herberg Vlissinghe PUB

18 🚇 MAP P42, F1

Luminaries have frequented Bruges' oldest pub for 500 years; local legend has it that Rubens once painted an imitation coin on the table here and then did a runner. The interior is gorgeously preserved with wood panelling and a wood-burning stove, but in summer the best seats are in the shady garden where you can play boules. (📞 050-34 37 37; www.cafevlissinghe.be; Blekersstraat 2; ⏰ 11am-10pm Wed-Sat, to 7pm Sun)

De Garre PUB

19 🚇 MAP P42, D4

Try the fabulous Garre draught beer, which comes with a thick floral head in a glass that's almost a brandy balloon; the pub will only serve you three of these as they're a head-spinning 11% alcohol. The hidden two-floor *estaminet* (tavern) also stocks dozens of other fine Belgian brews, including the remarkable Struise Pannepot (€3.50). (📞 050-34 10 29; www.degarre.be; De Garre 1; ⏰ noon-midnight Sun-Thu, to 12.30am Fri, 11am-12.30am Sat)

't Poatersgat PUB

20 🚇 MAP P42, C2

Look carefully for the concealed hole in the wall and follow the stair-case down into this cross-vaulted cellar glowing with ethereal white lights and flickering candles. 't Poatersgat (which means 'the Monk's Hole') has 120 Belgian beers on the menu, including a smashing selection of Trappists. (📞0495 22 68 50; Vlamingstraat 82; 🕙3pm-late)

De Windmolen
PUB

21 🚇 MAP P42, G1

Quaint corner *café* with a sunny terrace overlooking one of the St-Anna windmills. (📞050-33 97 39; Carmersstraat 135; 🕙10am-10pm Mon-Thu, to 1am Fri-Sun)

Rose Red
BAR

22 🚇 MAP P42, D3

Outstanding beers from 50 of the best breweries in Belgium, served by charming and informa-tive staff in this pink-hued and rose-scattered bar. There are five to six beers on tap and 150 bottles, or you can taste four beers for €10. (📞050-33 90 51; www.cordoeanier.be/en/rosered.php; Cordoeaniersstraat 16; 🕙11am-11pm Tue-Sun)

Merveilleux Tearoom
CAFE

23 🚇 MAP P42, B4

An elegant marble-floored tearoom on a cobbled passage near Markt. Coffee comes with a dainty homemade biscuit and sometimes a little glass of straw-berry ice cream or chocolate mousse. Pretty cakes and tea are on offer too. (📞050-61 02 09; www.merveilleux.eu; Muntpoort 8; 🕙10am-6pm)

Bruges Markt, Burg & North Bruges

't Brugs Beertje (p50)

KATE HOCKENHULL/ALAMY STOCK PHOTO ©

De Republiek
COCKTAIL BAR

24 MAP P42, B3

Set around a courtyard comprising characterful brick buildings, this big buzzing space is super-popular with Bruggelingen (Bruges locals). DJs hit the decks on Friday and Saturday nights. There's a long cocktail list, plus a range of well-priced meals (including vegetarian options) available until midnight. (📞050-73 47 64; http://republiek brugge.be; St-Jakobsstraat 36; ⊗noon-1am Wed-Sun, from 5pm Mon-Tue)

Du Phare
TAVERNA

25 MAP P42, E1

Tucked into what was one of Bruges' original town gates, this off-the-beaten-track tavern is best known for its live blues and jazz sessions

– check the website for dates. Bus 4 stops out the front. (📞050-34 35 90; www.duphare.be; Sasplein 2; ⊗bar 11.30am-late, kitchen 11.30am-3pm & 6pm-midnight Wed-Mon)

't Brugs Beertje
PUB

26 MAP P42, B5

Legendary throughout Bruges, Belgium and beyond for its hundreds of Belgian brews, this cosy *bruin café* (brown cafe) is filled with old advertising posters and locals who are part of the furniture. It's one of those perfect beer bars with smoke-yellowed walls, enamel signs, hop-sprig ceilings and knowledgeable staff to help you choose from a book full of brews. (📞050-33 96 16; www.brugsbeertje. be; Kemelstraat 5; ⊗4pm-midnight Mon, Thu & Sun, to 1am Fri & Sat)

Koninklijke Stadsschouwburg

PICS FACTORY/SHUTTERSTOCK ©

Belgian Chocolate Explained

Chocolate is fundamentally a mix of cocoa paste, sugar and cocoa butter in varying proportions. Dark chocolate uses the most cocoa paste, milk chocolate mixes in milk powder, and white chocolate uses cocoa butter but no cocoa paste at all. Mouth-watering Belgian chocolate is arguably the world's best because it sticks religiously to these pure ingredients, while other countries allow cheaper vegetable fats to replace some of the cocoa butter. The essential Belgian chocs are pralines and creamy *manons* – filled bite-sized chocolates sold from an astonishing range of specialist shops. Here glove-clad assistants wrap whatever you select from the enchanting display – it's fine to buy just a single chocolate. Price varies radically according to the brand.

Entertainment

Koninklijke Stadsschouwburg THEATRE

27 ⭐ MAP P42, C3

Cultuurcentrum Brugge coordinates theatrical and concert events at several venues, including this majestic 1869 theatre. Opera, classical concerts, theatre and dance are on offer. Out front is a statue of Papageno from Mozart's *The Magic Flute*. (📞050-44 30 60; www.ccbrugge.be; Vlamingstraat 29)

Retsin's Lucifernum LIVE MUSIC

28 ⭐ MAP P42, E3

A former Masonic lodge owned by a self-proclaimed vampire. Ring the bell on a Sunday night, pass the voodoo temple and hope you're invited inside, where you might be serenaded with live Latin music and an otherworldly candle-lit bar may be serving potent rum cocktails. It's always a surprise. Don't miss the graves in the tropical garden. (📞0476 35 06 51; www.lucifernum.be; Twijnstraat 6-8; admission incl drink €10; ⏰8-11pm Sun)

Cultuurcentrum Brugge THEATRE

29 ⭐ MAP P42, B3

This cultural group organises theatre productions, events and concerts and coordinates performances at the Koninklijke Stadsschouwburg and **Magdalenazaal** (MaZ; Magdalenastraat 27). Check the website for what's on where and when. (📞info 050- 44 30 40, tickets 050-44 30 60; www.ccbrugge.be; St-Jakobsstraat 20)

Cinema Lumière CINEMA

30 ⭐ MAP P42, B3

Just a couple of blocks back from Markt, this art-house cinema

Laced Up – The Art of Making Lace

There are two main ways of making lace (*kant*/*dentelle* in Dutch/French). Needlepoint lace (*naaldkant*) uses a single thread to embroider a pattern on a piece of cloth or paper that will eventually be discarded. Originally Italian, the technique was perfected in Brussels, and the classic needlepoint stitch is still known as 'corded Brussels'.

In contrast, bobbin lace (*kloskant*) creates a web of interlinked threads using multiple threaded-bobbins meticulously twisted using a maze of hand-placed pins. It's an astonishingly fiddly process, believed to have originated in 14th-century Bruges. Some of the finest handmade samples, made using hundreds of bobbins, originated in Binche, while Chantilly, an originally French subform using black cotton, was for years a noted speciality craft of Geraardsbergen.

These days much lace-making is mechanised, but the handmade craft can still be seen at Bruges' **Kantcentrum** (Map p42, G1; Lace Centre; ☏050-33 00 72; http://kantcentrum.eu; Balstraat 16; adult/child €5/4; ☻10am-5pm). Lace makes a great Bruges souvenir.

---

screens a well-chosen program of foreign films in their original language. (☏050-34 34 65; www.lumierecinema.be; St-Jakobsstraat 36b; ☻noon-11pm)

Shopping

Chocolate Line CHOCOLATE

31 🏠 MAP P42, B5

Bruges has 50 chocolate shops, but just five where chocolates are handmade on the premises. Of those, the Chocolate Line is the brightest and best. Wildly experimental flavours by 'shock-o-latier' Dominique Persoone include bitter Coca-Cola, Cuban cigar, wasabi, and black olive, tomato and basil.

It also sells pots of chocolate body paint, complete with a brush. (☏050-82 01 26; www.thechocolateline.be; Simon Stevinplein 19; per kg €50; ☻10am-6pm)

De Reyghere Reisboekhandel BOOKS

32 🏠 MAP P42, C4

This fabulously well-stocked travel bookshop is an extension of **De Reyghere Boekhandel** next door; it's been in the same family for generations. Past shoppers include Albert Einstein. (☏050-33 34 03; www.reisboekhandel.be; Markt 13; ☻9.30am-noon Tue-Sat & 2-6pm Mon-Sat)

Galler
CHOCOLATE

33 🔒 MAP P42, C4

Chocoholics will be in heaven in this boutique chocolatier just off Markt. (📞050-61 20 62; www.galler.com; Steenstraat 5; ⏱10am-5.30pm)

Vismarkt
MARKET

34 🔒 MAP P42, E4

The stone slabs of the colonnaded 1821 fish market still accommodate fish stalls most mornings, along with trinket sellers later in the day. Several seafood restaurants here back onto pretty Huidenvettersplein, where archetypal Bruges buildings include the old tanners' guildhouse. (Fish Market; Vismarkt; ⏱7am-1pm Tue-Fri)

2-Be
FOOD & DRINKS

35 🔒 MAP P42, D5

Vast range of Belgian products from beers to biscuits in a snazzy, central location, but prices can be exorbitant. Their 'beer wall' is worth a look, as is the wonderfully located canal-side bar terrace, where 'monster' 3L draught beers (€19.50) are surely Belgium's biggest. (📞050-61 12 22; www.2-be.biz; Wollestraat 53; ⏱10am-7pm)

Rombaux
MUSIC

36 🔒 MAP P42, E3

Here since 1920, this large, family-run music shop specialises in classical, jazz, Flemish, folk and world music, and is the kind of place where you can browse for hours. It also sells sheet music and acoustic guitars. (📞050-33 25 75; www.rombaux.be; Mallebergplaats 13; ⏱2-6.30pm Mon, 10am-12.30pm & 2-6.30pm Tue-Fri, 10am-6pm Sat)

Olivier Strelli
FASHION & ACCESSORIES

37 🔒 MAP P42, A6

Belgium's best-known designer, who has an emphasis on colourful scarves, shoes and watches. (📞050-34 38 37; https://strelli.be; Zuidzandstraat 11-13; ⏱10am-6pm Mon-Sat)

Explore ✦
South Bruges

Bruges may strike visitors as being somewhat like an open-air museum, particularly in this area, where the historical buildings, galleries and churches cluster. True, Bruges' harmonious Gothic architecture, willow-lined waterways and market-filled squares are almost impossibly quaint. But beyond the souvenir shops you'll find cosy backstreet bars and cafés (pubs), young artisans and a palpable sense of history.

To escape the crowds, head south of Markt to where the tightly-knit central warren of lanes and alleys widens out into broader streets, with a greater concentration of 'real-life' businesses and restaurants frequented by locals. Also here are some of the city's most interesting museums, including the world-class Groeningemuseum (p56) art gallery and the unique Museum Sint-Janshospitaal (p58). A little further south, you'll find Bruges' begijnhof (p60) and its calm courtyard, the local favourite Koningin Astridpark (p63) and the romantic Minnewater Park (p61) with its pretty flowerbeds, before strolling back to Markt via the city vests, where you can even spot a working windmill or two.

Getting There & Around

🚌 Departing from Bruges' bus station, catch any Centrum-bound bus to Markt, from where it's generally only a few minutes' walk south to most attractions.

Neighbourhood Map on p64

Minnewater (p61) with Onze-Lieve-Vrouwekerk (p66) in the background PREDRAG JANKOVIC/SHUTTERSTOCK ©

Top Sight 📷
Groeningemuseum

Bruges' most celebrated art gallery boasts an astonishingly rich collection that's strong in superb Flemish Primitive and Renaissance works, depicting the conspicuous wealth of the city with glittering realistic artistry. There are some intriguing early images of Bruges itself, an eye-popping Hieronymus Bosch and more meditative works by Van Eyck and Memling. Later artists featured include Khnopff, Magritte and Delvaux.

◉ MAP P64, E2

☏ 050-44 87 11

www.visitbruges.be/en/ groeningemuseum- groeninge-museum

Dijver 12

adult/concession/under 18yr €12/10/free

⊙ 9.30am-5pm Tue-Sun

City as Patron

The gallery gets underway with absorbing images of Bruges commissioned by its merchant patrons. A map – more like an aerial view – shows 15th-century Bruges in every detail, from spinning windmills to tall ships in the harbour. Gerard David's grisly Judgement of Cambyses (1498) also features the cityscape.

Flemish Primitives

Things take off artistically in the Flemish Primitives room, crammed with works by Jan Van Eyck, Roger Van der Weyden, Hans Memling and Gerard David. These pieces depict the conspicuous wealth of the city with glittering realistic artistry.

Typical is the *Madonna Crowned by Angels* (1482) by the Master of the Embroidered Foliage, where the rich fabric of the Madonna's robe meets the 'real' foliage at her feet with exquisite detail, and Van Eyck's *Madonna with Canon Van der Paele* (1436). Van Eyck's portraits, like those of his counterparts, reflect the abundance of the city at that time, while adding a further dimension of psychological realism.

Townscapes & Landscapes

Visions of the city surface again in this room, with picturesque scenes by Jan Anton Garemijn, as well as Auguste Van de Steene's austere view of Markt.

Flemish Art: from Expressionism to Surrealism

These works from the 1920s show the influence of cubism and German expressionism on Flemish artists – most striking are Constant Permeke's earth-coloured depictions of peasant life in *Man Eating Milk-Soup* and *Angelus*. Two further rooms also cover the modern period, ending with works from the '60s and '70s, which show the influence of arch-surrealist Magritte.

★ Top Tips

o As with many Belgian attractions, the museum is closed on Monday.

o The museum is justifiably popular, so arrive as early as possible at busy times of year.

o If you're short on time, focus on works by the Flemish Primitives, which are the highlight of the museum.

o You'll notice the work of the 'primitives' is actually pretty sophisticated – the name derives from the Latin primus (first), as the artists were the first to adopt new painting techniques.

✕ Take a Break

A short walk along the canal from the museum brings you to stylish Den Dyver (p69), serving top-quality Belgian cuisine.

For something a little more low-key and easier on the budget, head to the fabulously friendly Books and Brunch (p70).

Top Sight 📷
Museum Sint-Janshospitaal

In the restored chapel of a 12th-century hospital building with superb timber beamwork, this museum shows various medical artefacts. But it's much better known for its six masterpieces by 15th-century artist Hans Memling, including the enchanting reliquary of St Ursula, which looks like a miniature Gothic cathedral.

◎ MAP P64, D3

📞 050-44 87 43

www.visitbruges.be/en/
sint-janshospitaal-saint
-johns-hospital

Mariastraat 38

adult/concession/under
18yr €12/10/free

🕙 9.30am-5pm Tue-Sun

Memling Paintings

The old hospital chapel houses **Memling-museum**, with a small but priceless collection of works by Hans Memling, which glow in the dim light. Largest is the triptych of St John the Baptist and St John the Evangelist, commissioned by the hospital church as an altarpiece. Look out for St Catherine (with spinning wheel) and St Barbara, both seated at the feet of the Virgin. Memling's secular portraits are just as engrossing as the devotional work, such as the delicate *Portrait of a Young Woman* (1480), where the subject's hands rest on the painted frame of her portrait.

Reliquary of St Ursula

This gilded oak reliquary (pictured) looks like a miniature Gothic cathedral. It was painted by Memling with scenes from the life of St Ursula, including highly realistic Cologne cityscapes. The devout Ursula was a Breton princess betrothed to a pagan prince. She agreed to marry him on the condition that she could make a pilgrimage to Rome (via Cologne) with 11,000 virgins. All were murdered on the return journey by the king of the Huns, along with Ursula and her betrothed.

Sint-Janshospitaal Artefacts

The lofty Sint-Janshospitaal has been elegantly restored to show off both the exposed beams of the 12th-century building and an array of artefacts relating to the museum. The latter includes tortuous-looking medical implements, hospital sedan chairs and a gruesome 1679 painting of an anatomy class.

★ Top Tips

o The museum shop has excellent in-depth guides to the exhibits and paintings.

o Though it's not the main event, the 17th-century *apotheek* (pharmacy) is worth a look. It's a beautiful tiled space with rows of jars and a pendulum clock.

o Take a peek into the Trustees Room, adjoining the pharmacy. It's lined with portraits of bewigged and beruffled trustees.

✕ Take a Break

Head down Maria-straat until it turns into Katelijnestraat, and enjoy the vegie offerings of De Bron (p69).

Pop into the Brouwerij De Halve Maan (p66) *café* for the finest local brew – hopping on an excellent 45-minute brewery tour is optional.

Top Sight 📷
Begijnhof

Bruges' delightful begijnhof dates from the 13th century. Despite the hordes of summer tourists, it remains a remarkably tranquil haven. Outside the 1776 gateway bridge lies a tempting (if predictably tourist-priced) array of terraced restaurants, lace shops and waffle peddlers.

◉ **MAP P64, C5**

Wijngaardstraat

admission free

🕑 6.30am-6.30pm

Ten Wijngaarde

This charming **17th-century house** (☎050-33 00 11; Begijnhof 24-28-30; adult/senior/child €2/€1.50/€1; ☉10am-5pm Mon-Sat, 2.30-5pm Sun) is now a domestic museum. In the rustic kitchen with blue-and-white Delft tiles you'll see a Louvain stove that extends into the room from the hearth so that people could sit around it. The sitting room displays black Chantilly lace, while the austere bedroom has a portrait showing a traditional *begijn* costume. The dining room features a simple wooden cupboard which served as a pantry, china store and pull-out dining table; beyond the house is a simple stone cloister with a well.

Church of the Beguinage

The baroque church features a flamboyant high altar, 17th-century choir stalls, and chubby cherubs adorning the choir screen. Outside, tall elm trees frame the view of the whitewashed houses, and despite the occasional crowds there's still a secluded, village-like air to the place.

Minnewater

Opposite the *begijnhof* is **Minnewater** (Map p64, D6) canal – known unofficially as the 'Lake of Love' – adjacent to a charming park of the same name. The romantic area has plenty of sheltered paths and benches to retreat to on a sunny day. In Bruges' medieval heyday, this is where ships from far and wide would unload their cargoes of wool, wine, spices and silks.

★ Top Tips

o Outside the *begijnhof*'s 1776 gateway bridge lies a tempting array of restaurants and waffle stands: handy if you want a snack, though prices are on the high side.

o Nearby Minnewater is a good location for a picnic.

o Photograph the *begijnhof* at dawn or dusk for maximum tranquility and good light.

✗ Take a Break

Stroll down a tranquil backstreet to delightful De Stoepa (p69), for bistro food and a pleasant hippy vibe.

For authentic pan-Asian flavours, Marco Polo Noodle Bar (p70) won't disappoint your taste buds (or break your budget).

Bruges' Parks & Canals

Head south when you feel the need to escape the crowds and find yourself a peaceful little spot to rest your weary legs, contemplate the scale of the historical magic you've just seen and recharge your batteries to tackle the next medieval adventure that lies just around the corner.

Walk Facts

Start Vismarkt

End Vismarkt

Length 3.2km; two to three hours

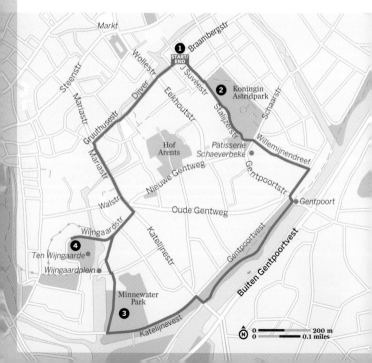

❶ Vismarkt

The handsome colonnaded 1821 fish market (p53) is still open for business most days. Fishmongers have been selling their North Sea produce here for centuries, though these days only a few vendors set up on the cold stone slabs. Join locals buying snacks such as *maatjes* (herring fillets). Check out pretty Huidenvettersplein, ringed with archetypal Bruges buildings.

❷ Koningin Astridpark

Walk south along Jozef Suvée-straat for a few minutes until you reach local hang-out **Koningin Astridpark**, named after the Swedish wife of King Léopold of Belgium; you'll come across her bust when you reach the park. Walk through the park, pass the Gothic revival Magdalen Church and you'll reach the scrumptious **Patisserie Schaeverbeke** (📞050-33 31 82; www.schaeverbeke.be; Schaarstraat 2; pastries from €2; ⏰7.30am-7pm Fri-Wed).

❸ Minnewater Park

Continue south to **Gentpoort** (📞050-44 87 11; www.visitbruges.be/en/gentpoort-gate-of-ghent; Gentpoortvest; adult/child/under 18yr

€4/3/free; ⏰9.30am-12.30pm & 1.30-5pm), one of the town's four medieval gateways. From here, a pleasant footpath leads through the greenery along the water's edge. Follow the path west until you reach Minnewater (p61)and its eponymous park, a scenic green space with orderly flower beds and secluded paths.

❹ Begijnhof

Just north of the park, **Wijngaard-plein**, a touristy but still irresistible square, is ringed by *cafés* (pubs). Look out for the horse fountain – the sculpted horses' heads spurt water, allowing carriage-drivers to fill buckets and give their horses a drink. The *cafés* here are a little on the pricey side, but the views are refreshing. Over the little arched bridge from the square, the 13th-century Begijnhof (p60) is one of the delights of Bruges, its whitewashed buildings encircling a garden with tall trees and swathes of daffodils in spring. It's well worth visiting Ten Wijngaarde (p61), the house museum here, as well as the church.

Wind your way back to Vismarkt via Wijngaardstraat, Mariastraat, Gruuthusestraat and Dijver.

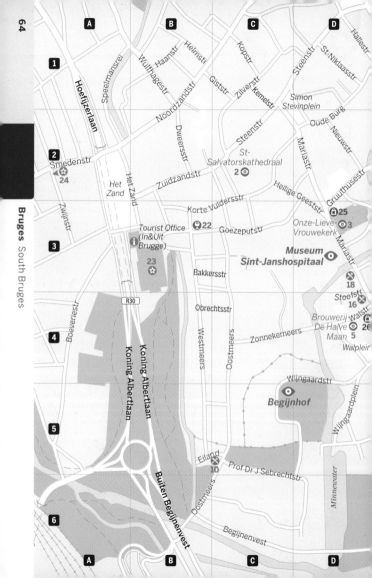

1

A **B** **C** **D**

Speelmansrei
Wulfhagestr
Haanstr
Helmstr
Giststr
Kopstr
Steenstr
St-Niklaasstr
Hallestr

Hoefijzerlaan

Noordzandstr
Dweersstr
Zilverstr
Kemelstr
Simon
Stevinplein
Oude Burg
Nieuwstr

2
Smedenstr
24
Steenstr
St-
Salvatorskathedraal
2
Mariastr
Gruuthusestr

Het
Zand
Het Zand
Zuidzandstr
Heilige Geeststr
25

Zwijnstr
Korte Vuldersstr
22
Goezeputstr
Onze-Lieve-
Vrouwekerk
3
Mariastr

3
Tourist Office
(In&Uit
Brugge)
23

Museum
Sint-Janshospitaal
18

Bakkersstr
Stoofstr
16

Boeveriestr
Obrechtsstr
Westmeers
Oostmeers
Zonnekemeers
Brouwerij
De Halve
Maan 5
Walstr
26
Walplein

4

R30

Koning Albertlaan
Koning Albertlaan

Wijngaardstr

Begijnhof

Wijngaardplein

5

Buiten Begijnenvest

Eiland
10
Prof Dr J Sebrechtstr

Minnewater

6
Oostmeers
Begijnenvest

A **B** **C** **D**

E

F

G

H

Wollestr

Huiden-
vettersplein

Bruges
Canal Tours **1**

21

Braambergstr

Freren Fonteinstr

Waalsestr

17 ✕
19 ✕

Schaarstr

1

Rozenhoedkaai

't Pandreitje

20

Park

Minderbroederstr

Engelstraat

Coupure

Dijver

✕**9**

Eekhoutstr

Koningin
Astridpark

Stalijzerstr

11
✕

2

◎ **Groeningemuseum**

4
◎ Arentshuis

6 ◎ Hof Arents

Garenmarkt

15
✕

Schaarstr

Gapaardstr

St-Bonifaciusbrug
✕**12**

Hof
Arents

14
✕

Nieuwe Gentweg

Willemijnendreef

3

Kastanjeboomstr

Groeninge

Nieuwe Gentweg

Gentpoortstr

Godshuis St-Jozef
7 ◎ & De Meulenaere

8
◎ Diamantmuseum

Oude Gentweg

4

Katelijnestr

13 ✕

Noordstr

Gentpoortvest

Buiten Gentpoortvest

5

Sulferbergstr

Katelijnestr

For reviews see	
◎ Top Sights	p56
◎ Sights	p66
✕ Eating	p69
🍷 Drinking	p71
★ Entertainment	p72
🔒 Shopping	p73

Minnewater
Park

Katelijnevest

Ⓝ
0 ⸻ 200 m
0 ⸻ 0.1 miles

6

E

F

G

H

Sights

Bruges Canal Tours
BOATING

1 MAP P64, E1

The must-do activity in Bruges is to see the city by water on a 30-minute canal boat tour. Boats depart roughly every 20 minutes from jetties south of Burg, including Rozenhoedkaai and Dijver. Each operator is essentially a branch of one or two companies regulated by the city: they all do the loop, they all cost the same. (adult/child €8/4; ⏱10am-6pm Mar–mid-Nov)

St-Salvators kathedraal
CATHEDRAL

2 MAP P64, C2

Stacked sub-towers top the massive central tower of 13th-century St Saviour's Cathedral. In daylight the construction looks somewhat dour, but once floodlit at night, it takes on a mesmerising fascination. The cathedral's interior is vastly high but feels oddly plain despite a selection of antique tapestries. Beneath the tower, a glass floor reveals some painted graves, and there's a passingly interesting **treasury** displaying 15th-century brasses and a 1559 triptych by Dirk Bouts. (☎050-33 68 41; Sint-Salvatorskoorstraat 8; treasury adult/child €2/1; ⏱2-5.45pm Mon, 9am-noon & 2-5.45pm Tue-Fri, 9am-noon & 2-3.30pm Sat & Sun, treasury 2-5pm Sun-Fri)

Onze-Lieve-Vrouwekerk
CHURCH

3 MAP P64, D3

Dominating its surrounds, this 13th-century church was reopened in 2015 after extensive renovations. Its enormous 115m spire is unmissable throughout much of the city. Inside, it's best known for Michelangelo's serenely contemplative 1504 *Madonna and Child* statue, the only such work by Michelangelo to leave Italy during the artist's lifetime. Look out also for the *Adoration of the Shepherds* by Pieter Pourbus. (Church of Our Lady; Mariastraat; adult/concession/under 18yr €6/5/free; ⏱9.30am-5pm Mon-Sat, from 1.30pm Sun)

Arentshuis
GALLERY

4 MAP P64, E2

This stately 18th-century patrician house displays the powerful paintings and dark-hued etchings of Frank Brangwyn (1867–1956), a Bruges-born artist of Welsh parentage. His images of WWI – he was an official war artist – are particularly powerful. Admission is free with your Groeningemuseum (p56) ticket. (☎050-44 87 11; Dijver 16; adult/concession/child €4/3/free; ⏱9.30am-5pm Tue-Sun)

Brouwerij De Halve Maan
BREWERY

5 MAP P64, D4

Founded in 1856, though there has been a brewery on the site since 1564, this is the last family *brouwerij* (brewhouse) in central Bruges. Multilingual, 45-minute **guided visits** (€8; 11am to 4pm, to 5pm Saturday) depart on the hour. These include a tasting but can sometimes be rather crowded. Alternatively, you can simply sip one of their excellent *Brugse Zot* (Bruges Fool, 7%) or *Straffe Hendrik* (Strong Henry, 9%) beers in the appealing brewery *café*. (☎050-33 26 97; www.halvemaan.be; Walplein 26; admission free; ⏱10.30am-6pm, closed mid-Jan)

Hof Arents

PARK

6 ◎ MAP P64, E2

Behind the Arentshuis (p66), Hof Arents is a charming little park with a hump-backed pedestrian bridge, **St-Bonifaciusbrug** (Map p64, E3), that crosses the canal,

offering idyllic views. Nicknamed Lovers' Bridge, it's where many a Bruges citizen steals their first kiss. Privileged guests staying at the **Guesthouse Nuit Blanche** (☎0494 40 04 47; www.bb-nuit blanche.com; Groeninge 2; d from €185; P ❄ 🛜) get the romantic moonlit scene all to themselves once the park has closed. (⏱7am-10pm Apr-Sep, to 9pm Oct-Mar)

Godshuis St-Jozef & De Meulenaere

HISTORIC BUILDING

7 ◎ MAP P64, E4

These almshouses offer one of the city's most spacious oases of calm; enter via the green door. (Nieuwe Gentweg 24; admission free; ⏱10am-4pm)

St-Bonifaciusbrug

ALXCR5/SHUTTERSTOCK ©

Begijnhoven & Godshuizen

In the 12th century, large numbers of men from the Low Countries embarked on crusades to the Holy Land and never returned. Their unchaperoned women-folk often felt obliged to seek security by joining a religious order. However, joining a convent required giving up one's worldly possessions and even one's name. A middle way, especially appealing to relatively wealthy widows, was to become a *begijn* (*béguine* in French).

These lay sisters made Catholic vows including obedience and chastity, but could maintain their private wealth. They lived in a self-contained *begijnhof* (*béguinage* in French): a cluster of houses built around a central garden and church, surrounded by a protective wall. Land (normally at the outskirts of town) was typically granted by a pious feudal lord, but once established these all-female communities were self-sufficient. Most had a farm and vegetable garden and made supplementary income from lace-making and from benefactors who would pay the *begijnen* to pray for them.

In the 16th century, Holland's growing Protestantism meant that most Dutch *begijnhoven* were swept away. But Spanish-ruled Flanders was gripped by a fervently Catholic Counter-Reformation that reshaped the *begijn* movement. Rebuilt *begijnhoven* became hospice-style institutions with vastly improved funding. From 1583 the Archbishop of Mechelen decreed a standardised rulebook and a nunlike 'uniform' for *begijnen*, who at one point comprised almost 5% of Flanders' female population.

Looking somewhat similar to *begijnhoven* but usually on a smaller scale are *godshuizen* (almshouses), typically featuring redbrick or whitewashed-shuttered cottages set around a tiny enclosed garden. Originally built by merchant guilds for their members or by rich sponsors to provide shelter for the poor (and to save the sponsors' souls), these days they're great places to peacefully unwind if you dare to push open their usually closed doors. Bruges has a remarkable 46 *godshuizen*.

Diamantmuseum   MUSEUM

8 MAP P64, E4

While Antwerp is now the centre of the diamond industry, the idea of polishing the stones with diamond 'dust' was originally pioneered in Bruges. This is the theme of this slick museum which also displays a lumpy greenish 252-carat raw diamond and explains how the catchphrase 'diamonds are forever' started as a De Beers marketing campaign. Diamond-polishing demonstrations (at 12.15pm and 3.15pm) cost €3 extra. (Diamond Museum; ☎050-34 20 56; www.diamondmuseum.be; Katelijnestraat 43; adult/senior/student €8/7/7, combined ticket with Choco-Story €14; ⏱10.30am-5.30pm)

Eating

Den Dyver BELGIAN €€€

9 ✕ MAP P64, E2

Den Dyver is a pioneer of fine beer dining where you match the brew you drink with the one the chef used to create the sauce on your plate. This is no pub: beers come in wine glasses served on starched tablecloths in an atmosphere of Burgundian grandeur. The lunch menu includes *amuse-bouche*, nibbles and coffee. (☎050-33 60 69; www.dyver.be; Dijver 5; mains €23-47, tasting menu €45; ⏱noon-2pm & 6.30-9.30pm Fri-Mon)

De Stoepa BISTRO €€

10 ✕ MAP P64, C5

A gem of a place in a peaceful residential setting. It's got a slightly hippie/Buddhist ambience; oriental statues, terracotta-coloured walls, a metal stove and wooden floors and furniture give a homey but stylish feel. Best of all is the leafy terrace garden. Tuck into the up-market bistro-style food. (☎050-33 04 54; www.stoepa.be; Oostmeers 124; mains €12-26; ⏱noon-2pm & 6pm-midnight Tue-Sat, noon-3pm & 6-11pm Sun)

Pomperlut BELGIAN €€

11 ✕ MAP P64, H2

Opposite the lovely Koningin Astrid-park, with a fine outdoor terrace and a cosy dark-wood interior, this popular bistro serves traditional Belgian food and beer. It has particularly friendly, welcoming staff. (☎050-70 86 26; www.pomperlut.be; Minderbroedersstraat 26; mains €14-22; ⏱6am-10pm Tue-Sat)

Den Gouden Harynck INTERNATIONAL €€€

12 ✕ MAP P64, E3

Behind an ivy-clad facade, this uncluttered Michelin-starred restaurant garners consistent praise and won't hurt the purse quite as severely as some better-known competitors. Its lovely location is both central and secluded. Exquisite dishes might include noisettes of venison topped with lardo and quince purée, or seed-crusted fillet of bream. (☎050-33 76 37; www.goudenharynck.be; Groeninge 25; set lunch menu €45, midweek dinner €65, surprise menu €95; ⏱noon-1.30pm & 7-8.30pm Tue-Fri, 7-8.30pm Sat)

De Bron VEGETARIAN €

13 ✕ MAP P64, E4

By the time this glass-roofed restaurant's doors open, a queue has usually formed outside, full of diners keen to get vegetarian fare direct from *de bron* (the source). Dishes are available in small, medium and large, and there are some delicious soups, such as pumpkin. Vegans are catered for on request. (📞050-33 45 26; Katelijnestraat 82; snacks from €6; 🕙11.45am-2pm Mon-Fri; 🍴)

Christophe
BISTRO €€

14 🍴 MAP P64, F3

A cool late-night bistro with marble tabletops and a decent range of Flemish staples including fresh Zeebrugge shrimps. (📞050-34 48 92; www.christophe-brugge.be; Garenmarkt 34; mains €19-32; 🕙6pm-1am Thu-Mon)

Books and Brunch
CAFE €€

15 🍴 MAP P64, F2

This fabulous little cafe with exceptionally friendly and helpful staff is the perfect place to start your day, whether you're a late starter or an early riser. Tucked away from the crowds, and a short stroll to loved-by-locals Koningin Astridpark, you're surrounded by pre-loved books in Dutch and English, all of which are for sale. (📞050-70 90 79; Garenmarkt 30; mains €8-18; 🕙9am-3pm)

Marco Polo Noodle Bar
NOODLES €

16 🍴 MAP P64, D4

You can't beat this always-cramped little noodle bar for its wide range of Asian flavours, from pho to ramen and dumplings too. Great value. It's just outside the centre. (📞050-73 42 85; www.marco-polo-noodles.com; Katelijnestraat 29; noodle soups €9-14; 🕙noon-3.30pm & 5-9.30pm)

Resto Ganzespel
BELGIAN €€

17 🍴 MAP P64, H1

Providing a truly intimate eating experience in a lovely old gabled building, the owner serves classic Belgian dishes such as meatballs and *kalfsblanket* (veal in a creamy sauce), as well as pasta dishes. Upstairs are three idiosyncratic B&B guest rooms (doubles €55 to €85), one with a musical shower. (📞050-33 12 33; www.ganzespel. be; Ganzenstraat 37; mains €12-21; 🕙6.30-10pm Sat & Sun)

De Proeverie
CAFE €

18 🍴 MAP P64, D3

A chintzy but appealing tearoom serving a variety of teas, gloopy hot chocolate, milkshakes and indulgent homemade sweets including crème brûlée, chocolate mousse and *merveilleux* cake. Coffee comes with generous goodies on the side. (📞050-33 08 87; www. sukerbuyc.be; Katelijnestraat 5-6; snacks from €5; 🕙9.30am-6pm)

In 't Nieuwe Museum
BELGIAN €€

19 🍴 MAP P64, H1

So called because of the museum-like collection of brewery plaques, money boxes and other mementos of *café* life adorning the walls, this family-owned local favourite serves succulent meat cooked in a 17th-century open-fire oven.

Specials include vegie burgers, eel dishes, ribs, steaks and creamy *vispannetje* (fish casserole). (☎050-33 12 80; www.nieuw-museum.com; Hooistraat 42; mains €17-26; ◷6-11pm Fri-Tue, plus 12.30-2.30pm Sun)

Drinking

L'Estaminet   PUB

20 🚇 MAP P64, F1

With its dark-timber beams, low lighting, convivial clatter and park setting, L'Estaminet scarcely seems to have changed since it opened in 1900. It's primarily a drinking spot, but also serves time-honoured dishes such as spaghetti bolognese with a baked cheese crust (€10). Summer sees its loyal local following flow out

onto the front terrace. (☎050-33 09 16; www.estaminet-brugge.be/en; Park 5; ◷noon-late)

't Klein Venetie   PUB

21 🚇 MAP P64, F1

Don't miss the superb canal view from outside this popular *café*. With the belfry towering above a perfect gaggle of medieval housefronts, the view is lovely any time, but it's especially compelling at dusk as the floodlights come on. (☎0475 72 52 25; www.kleinvenetie. be; Braambergstraat 1; ◷noon-midnight)

The Vintage   PUB

22 🚇 MAP P64, B3

Unusually hip for Bruges, with a '60s/'70s vibe and a vintage

Cupcakes at De Proeverie

Belgian Brews

Belgian beer is much more than a recipe for a good night out. Beer is to Belgium what wine is to neighbouring France – something to be savoured slowly, appreciating each brew's individual characteristics and flavours. Appreciating them all could take a while: it's estimated up to 1000 different beers are brewed nationwide. Each beer has its own unique glass embossed with the beer's logo (marking the level where the head starts) and is specially shaped to enhance the taste and aromas, meaning pouring techniques vary.

While monks in France are renowned for winemaking, in Belgium they're devoted to beer. Smooth gold- and dark-coloured Trappist beers – packing 6% to 12% alcohol content – have been made for centuries by Trappist (Cistercian) monks. These days, the monks' average age is 70, and there are few new recruits, prompting fears for the beers' future. For now, three abbeys still brew in Flanders.

In the same way that France has champagne, Belgium has its traditional vintage, the lambic (*lambiek* in Dutch). Like champagne, these sparkling beers take up to three years to make. The secret is wild microorganisms that inhabit the cold air around the beer, causing spontaneous fermentation. The most popular lambic is the cider-style *gueuze* (pronounced 'gerze'). They're an acquired taste, but beginners can try fruit lambics that are sweetened with cherry or raspberry.

Easier to wash down than lambic are pale, cloudy white beers (*witbier* in Dutch, *bière blanche* in French), such as Bruges' Brugs Tarwebier. These are great iced with lemon in warm weather, unlike many of the country's beers, which are actually best drunk at room temperature. Belgium also boasts golden ales; abbey beers (strong, full-flavoured ales, such as Leffe, using original abbey recipes); Vlaams Rood ('Flemish Red' beers, aged in wooden barrels); and sour-tasting Oud Bruin ('Old Brown' beers that blend young and old brews, with a secondary fermentation in the bottle).

Vespa hanging from the roof. The sunny terrace is a nice spot for a Jupiler, and the theme parties can be raucous. (☎050-34 30 63; www.facebook.com/TheVintageBrugge; Westmeers 13; ⏰11am-1am Thu-Tue)

Entertainment

Concertgebouw CONCERT VENUE

23 ⭐ MAP P64, B3

Bruges' stunning 21st-century concert hall is the work of architects Paul Robbrecht and Hilde Daem. It takes its design cues from the city's three famous towers and red bricks. Theatre, classical music and dance performances are regularly staged. The tourist office (p148) is situated at street level. (☎050-47 69 99; www.concertgebouw.be; Het Zand 34; ticket prices vary)

Cactus Muziekcentrum
LIVE MUSIC

24 ⭐ MAP P64, A2

Though small, this is the city's top venue for contemporary and world music, hosting both live bands and international DJs. It also organises festivals including the **Cactus Music Festival** (www.cactusfestival.be; ☺Jul), held in the Minnewater Park (p63) at the southern edge of the old city. (☎050-33 20 14; www.cactusmusic.be; Magdalenastraat 27)

Shopping

Zucchero
FOOD

25 🏠 MAP P64, D3

A fabulous sweets shop with eye-popping fuchsia decor. It sells umpteen varieties of fudge and candies, plus ice cream to go. Check out the candy sticks being hand-chopped by the young owners. (☎050-33 39 62; www.confiserie-zucchero.be; Mariastraat 18; ☺10am-6pm Tue-Sat, from 11am Sun)

De Striep
COMICS

26 🏠 MAP P64, D4

Look for Thibaut Vandorselaer's wonderful illustrated guides at this colourful comic shop. There's also a comprehensive collection of comics and graphic novels in Dutch, French and English. You'll find Bruges-set comics by the counter. (☎050-33 71 12; www.striepclub.be; Katelijnestraat 42; ☺10am-12.30pm & 1.30-7pm Tue-Sat, 2-6pm Sun)

Worth a Trip 📷
Belgian Coast

After a period of stasis, Belgium's seaside region is fast regaining popularity among locals and tourists as an 'it' destination. The 65km-long coastline is fronted by wide sand beaches, backed by dunes and dotted every few kilometres with resort towns. Out of season many towns can feel deserted, but with its regular events and conventions, hub-town Ostend keeps a lively vibe year-round. Other top picks are De Haan, Knokke-Heist and Bredene.

NMBS/SNCB (p144) runs trains between Brussels and Ostend. De Kusttram (coast tram; p144) runs along the coast between Knokke-Heist and De Panne/Adinkerke. Single tickets cost €3. Buy a day pass on board for €8 or in advance for €6.

Ostend

Bustling Ostend is primarily a domestic seaside resort. Along its remarkably wide sandy beach is a spacious promenade surveyed by shoulder-to-shoulder tearooms. But it's also rich in history. As a fortified port it was ravaged by a four-year siege (1600–04) as the last 'Belgian' city to refuse Spanish reconquest. Later it bloomed as one of Europe's most stylish seaside resorts. Most of that style disappeared during WWII when German occupying forces (re)built the remarkable Atlantikwall sea defences, but young blood is restoring the town's wealth of belle époque architecture and giving it a new lease of life.

Belle Époque De Haan

Prim and proper De Haan (Le Coq; pictured) is Belgium's most compact and engaging beach resort. Fanciful half-timbered hotels, quaint eateries and tasteful boutiques form an appealing knot around a cottage-style former tram station, which houses the tourist office. Head east of the La Pontinière park, to discover a whimsical world of historic mansions in sandswept lanes hiding among gently shifting dunes.

Paul Delvaux Museum

The **Delvaux Museum** (☎ 058 52 12 29; www.delvauxmuseum.com; Paul Delvauxlaan 42; adult/concession €8/6; ⏱10.30am-5.30pm Tue-Sun Apr-Sep, Thu-Sun Oct-Dec, closed Jan-Mar) occupies a pretty whitewashed cottage that was home and studio to Paul Delvaux (1897–1994), one of Belgium's most famous surrealist artists. Explore his warped take on perspective and dreamy evocations of the 'poetic subconscious'. From the Koksijde/St-Idesbald tram stop, walk west along the main road towards De Panne, then follow signs inland and left, around 1km total. The museum has a delightful garden cafe.

★ **Top Tips**

o Every settlement offers a wide selection of accommodation, but heavy bookings mean finding a room can still be hard in summer.

o Head just inland to Veurne to see a classic medieval Belgian square.

o Make a musical odyssey in Ostend, where Marvin Gaye wrote 'Sexual Healing'.

✕ **Take a Break**

Tearoom restaurants covering a wide range of styles and prices stand side-by-side along the promenade west of Ostend's Kursaal. There are plenty more seafood restaurants along Visserkaai. Market day is Thursday.

Brussels Neighbourhoods

Grand Place & Îlot Sacré (p79)
The geographical heart of Brussels, with dazzling medieval buildings and standout restaurants, theatres and music venues.

EU Quarter & Etterbeek (p125)
As well as being the gleaming centre of EU power, this district boasts a beautiful park and some fine museums.

Grand Place ○

Centre Belge de la Bande Dessinée

MIM ○

Musées ○
Royaux des Beaux-Arts

Parc du Cinquantenaire

Musée Art & Histoire ○

Royal Quarter (p107)
This stately district has a compelling cluster of museums, some lovely green spaces, and the city's best chocolatiers.

Musée Horta ○

Explore Brussels

Historic yet hip, bureaucratic yet bizarre, self-confident yet unshowy, Brussels is multicultural to its roots. Brussels' heart beats in the Grand Place, ringed by gold-trimmed, gabled houses built by merchant guilds, and flanked by the 15th-century Gothic town hall. The majestic Royal Quarter is home to the city's' premier museums, housed in some of the city's most magnificent buildings. The EU Quarter also offers plenty of sights to entice visitors

Explore

Grand Place & Îlot Sacré

Brussels' heart beats in the Grand Place, ringed by gold-trimmed, gabled houses built by merchant guilds, and flanked by the 15th-century Gothic town hall. In the 12th century this was used as a marketplace; the names of the surrounding lanes still evoke herbs, cheese and poultry. Nearby are glass-covered shopping arcades and that Brussels icon, Manneken Pis (p86).

Start your day at Grand Place (p80), with its splendid guild houses and Brussels City Museum (p87) and if you fancy, the Musée Mode & Dentelle (p86) for historic lace ware. Take a turn around the glorious Galeries St-Hubert (p86) in the footsteps of Victor Hugo, and if you're a cartoon fan, the Centre Belge de la Bande Dessinée (p82). Have a predinner beer at the irresistible Théâtre Royal de Toone (p97), then listen to some live piano as you dine at Le Cercle des Voyageurs (p91), near the iconic Manneken Pis. Round out your day with more live sounds at the Music Village (p96).

Getting There & Around

M This central area is easily accessed via metro stations De Brouckère, Gare Centrale and Rogier.

🚊 Bourse station sits between the Îlot Sacré and Ste-Catherine areas.

🚶 It's a dense but compact area: walking from sight to sight makes sense, and means you can check out the area's murals.

Neighbourhood Map on p84

Hôtel de Ville (p81) on Grand Place TELESNIUK/SHUTTERSTOCK ©

Top Sight 📷
Grand Place

Alive with classic cafés (pubs), the square takes on different auras at different times. Visit more than once, including at night, when the scene is magically illuminated. The focal point is the spired 15th-century city hall, but each of the antique guildhalls (mostly 1697–1705) has a charm of its own.

◎ MAP P84, E5

Ⓜ Gare Centrale

Hôtel de Ville

Built between 1444 and 1480, the splendid **Hôtel de Ville** (City Hall; ☎ visitors office 02-279 43 47; guided tours €5; ⊙ tours 3pm Wed year-round, 10am & 2pm Sun Apr-Sep) was almost the only building on the Grand Place to escape bombardment by the French in 1695. The creamy stone facade is covered with Gothic gargoyles and reliefs of nobility. On top of the soaring tall tower is a gilded statue of St Michel, Brussels' patron saint.

Houses & Guildhalls

Among the Grand Place's gorgeous buildings and guildhalls are the following, listed by street number and guild. **5, Archers:** La Louve (The She-Wolf) has a golden phoenix rising from the ashes, which signifies the rebirth of the Grand Place after the bombardment. **6, Boatmen:** Le Cornet (The Horn) has a stern-shaped gable. **9, Butchers:** Le Cygne (The Swan) hosted Karl Marx in 1847. **10, Brewers:** L'Arbre d'Or (The Golden Tree) features hop plants climbing the columns – two basement rooms house a small Brewery Museum.

Maison du Roi

This fanciful feast of neogothic arches, verdigris statues and mini-spires is bigger, darker and nearly 200 years younger than the surrounding guildhalls. Once a medieval bread market, the current masterpiece dates from 1873 and nowadays houses the Brussels City Museum (p87), featuring old maps, architectural relics and paintings. Don't miss Pieter Brueghel the Elder's 1567 *Cortège de Noces (Wedding Procession)*, and the 760-odd costumes – including an Elvis suit – belonging to Manneken Pis.

Dukes of Brabant Mansion

The mansion consists of six 1698 houses behind a single palatial facade reworked in 1882. Had the imperial governor had his way after 1695, the whole square would have looked like this.

★ Top Tips

○ Tours depart from the tourist office daily: 10am for a bike tour or 3pm for a city walking tour with the same company.

○ There are guided tours of the Hôtel de Ville in English.

○ There's a flower market on Monday, Wednesday and Friday mornings.

○ The Grand Place hosts everything from Christmas fairs to rock concerts, to the extraordinary biennial 'flower carpet' (August).

✕ Take a Break

Take time out for speculoos biscuits, tea and ice cream at historic Dandoy (p92), just off the Grand Place.

For something fancier, stay on the square and eat at **La Maison du Cygne** (☎ 02-511 82 44; www.lamaisonducygne.com; Rue Charles Buls 2; mains €38-65, menus from €65; ⊙ noon-2pm & 7-10pm Mon-Fri, 7-10pm Sat; Ⓜ Gare Centrale).

Top Sight 📷

Centre Belge de la Bande Dessinée

Belgium's national Comic Strip Centre is a studious look at the evolution of comics: how they're made, seminal artists and their creations, and contemporary comic-strip artists. And everyone should have at least a quick look at Victor Horta's 1906 light-filled glass-and-steel textile warehouse in which the museum is housed.

◎ MAP P84, H2

☏ 02-219 19 80

www.comicscenter.net

Rue des Sables 20

adult/concession €10/7

🕙 10am-6pm

Ⓜ Rogier

The Invention of the Comic Strip

This exploration of the history of the ninth art goes right back to mosaics, and makes a compelling case that the manuscripts of medieval monks – with their divided story strips and speech bubbles – were the first cartoons. The revolution continues through to the picture stories of 19th-century New York newspapers.

The Museum of the Imagination

This gallery focuses on Belgium's favourite cartoon character, Tintin, created by the great Hergé. It posits Tintin as a visually blank 'everyman' who can transform himself into a granny, a turbaned Indian or a white-bearded sage. Volatile Captain Haddock is by contrast a volcano of uncontrolled emotion, while the narrative is often sparked by the misunderstandings and bizarre actions of Professor Calculus. Among other Belgian artists – explored in less depth – you may want to pause over the little blue creatures created by Peyo: the Smurfs.

Horta's Building

Designed as a department store in 1906, the lovely building features a swirling tiled floor, slim metal pillars, girders and grills and light filtered through a glass ceiling. As you enter, a model of Tintin's red rocket gleams against the pale stone; to the right is a small exhibition about the construction, decline and restoration of the building.

★ Top Tips

○ You don't have to pay an entrance fee to enjoy the central hallway or drink a coffee at the attached cafe.

○ Temporary exhibitions on the top floor show international comic-strip art.

○ Don't miss the shop, which steers clear of merchandise and focuses on books, including contemporary political satires.

○ Should you want more reading matter – albeit in French – there's a comic-book library next door.

✕ Take a Break

The adjoining cafe, **Brasserie Horta** (www.brasseriehorta. be; Rue des Sables 20; mains €14-18; ⏲ noon-3pm Tue-Sun), is an attractive place serving Belgian standards.

Otherwise take a stroll to the classic brasserie Arcadi (p90).

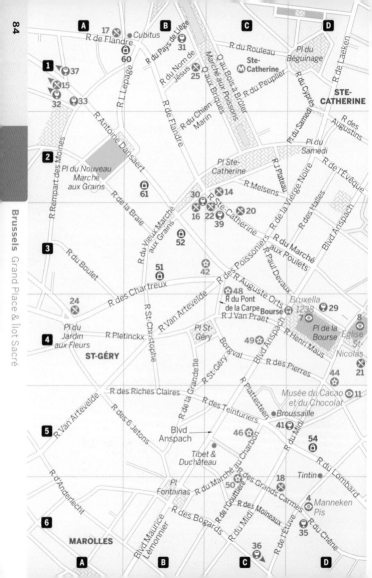

A

17 · Cubitus
R de Flandre
60
R L'Epage
R du Pays de Liège
R du Nom de Jésus

1
37
15
32 33

R Antoine Dansaert

2
Pl du Nouveau
Marché
aux Grains
61
R de la Braie

3
R du Boulet
R des Chartreux
52

R du Vieux Marché aux Grains

51
42

4
24
Pl du
Jardin
aux Fleurs
R Pletinckx
ST-GÉRY
R des Riches Claires
R St-Christophe
R Van Artevelde
Pl St-Géry

5
R Van Artevelde
R des 6 Jetons
R de la Grande Île
R St-Géry
Blvd
Anspach
Tibet &
Duchâteau
46
Pl
Fontainas

6
R d'Anderlecht
MAROLLES
Blvd Maurice Lemonnier
R des Bogards

B

Marché aux Poissons
31
25
R du Chien
Marin
Q au Bois à Brûler
Q aux Briques

Pl Ste-
Catherine
R Melsens

30 14
16 22 39
R Ste-Catherine

R des Poissonniers
R Auguste Orts
48
R du Pont
de la Carpe
Bourse
R J Van Praet
Borgval
49
R des Teinturiers
R de la Grande Île
R Plattesteen
54
41
R du Midi
50
18
R des Grands Carmes
R de Goutture
R des Moineaux
R du Midi
36
R de l'Étuve

C

R du Rouleau
Ste-
Catherine
R du Peuplier

Pl Ste-
Catherine
R J Plateau
R de la Vierge Noire

R du Marché aux Poulets
R Paul Devaux

Bruxella
1238
7
29

Pl de la
Bourse
R Henri Maus
R des Pierres
44
21
Musée du Cacao
et du Chocolat 11
Broussaille
R des Charbon
Tintin
4 Manneken
Pis
35
R du Chène

D

Pl du
Béguinage
R de Laeken

STE-
CATHERINE
R du Cyprès
Pl du
Samedi
R des
Augustins
R de l'Évêque
R des Halles
Blvd Anspach

Bourse

Église
St-
Nicolas
8

R du Lombard

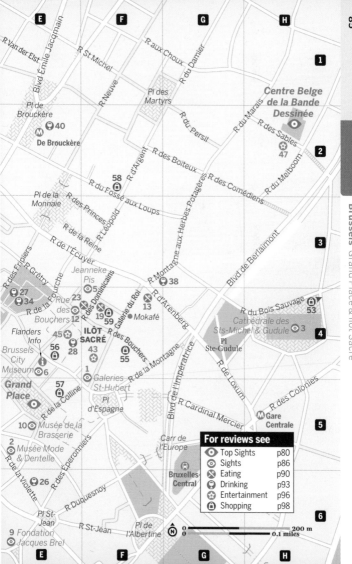

E   F   G   H

R Van der Elst

Blvd Émile Jacqmain

R St Michel

R aux Choux

R du Damier

Centre Belge de la Bande Dessinée

R Neuve

Pl des Martyrs

R du Persil

R du Marais

R des Sables

Pl de Brouckère

40

M De Brouckère

47

R d'Argent

R des Boiteux

R des Comédiens

58

R du Fossé aux Loups

R Montagne aux Herbes Potagères

R du Meiboom

Pl de la Monnaie

R des Princes

R de la Reine

R Léopold

R de l'Écuyer

Blvd de Berlaimont

R des Fripiers

R Grétry

Jeanneke Pis

38

R des Dominicains

R du Roi

R d'Arenberg

27

34

5

23

13

Mokafé

R des Bouchers

ÎLOT SACRÉ

19

59

R du Bois Sauvage

53

Cathédrale des Sts-Michel & Gudule

3

Pl Ste-Gudule

45

56

28

43

55

12

Rue des Bouchers

R de la Fourche

Flanders Info

Brussels City Museum

6

57

R de la Montagne

R de Loxum

Grand Place

R de la Colline

Galeries St-Hubert

Pl d'Espagne

Blvd de l'Impératrice

R Cardinal Mercier

R des Colonies

10 Musée de la Brasserie

M **Gare Centrale**

2 Musée Mode & Dentelle

R des Éperonniers

Carr de l'Europe

5

26

Bruxelles-Central

R de la Violette

Pl St-Jean

R St-Jean

R Duquesnoy

Pl de l'Albertine

9 Fondation Jacques Brel

N 0   200 m
0   0.1 miles

6

For reviews see	
⊙ Top Sights	p80
⊙ Sights	p86
✕ Eating	p90
⌾ Drinking	p93
☆ Entertainment	p96
⍟ Shopping	p98

Sights

Galeries St-Hubert ARCHITECTURE

1 ◉ MAP P84, F4

When opened in 1847 by King Léopold I, the glorious Galeries St-Hubert formed Europe's very first shopping arcade. Many enticing shops lie behind its neoclassical glassed-in arches flanked by marble pilasters. Several eclectic *cafés* spill tables onto the gallery terrace, safe from rain beneath the glass roof. The arcade is off Rue du Marché aux Herbes. (☏02-545 09 90; www.grsh.be; Rue du Marché aux Herbes; Ⓜ Gare Centrale)

Musée Mode & Dentelle MUSEUM

2 ◉ MAP P84, E5

Lace making has been one of Flanders' finest crafts since the 16th century. While *kloskant* (bobbin lace) originated in Bruges, *naaldkant* (needlepoint lace) was developed in Italy but was predominantly made in Brussels. This excellent museum reveals lace's applications for underwear and outerwear over the centuries, as well as displaying other luxury textiles in beautifully presented exhibitions. There's a new focus here on Belgium's ahead-of-the-curve fashion industry, with changing exhibitions of contemporary textiles. (Fashion & Lace Museum; ☏02-213 44 50; www.costumeandlacemuseum.brussels; Rue de la Violette 12; adult/child/BrusselsCard €8/free/free;

⊙10am-5pm Tue-Sun; Ⓜ Gare Centrale)

Cathédrale des Sts-Michel & Gudule CHURCH

3 ◉ MAP P84, H4

Host to coronations and royal weddings, Brussels' grand, twin-towered cathedral bears some resemblance to Paris' Notre Dame. Begun in 1226, construction took 300 years. Stained-glass windows flood the soaring nave with light, while column-saints brandish gilded tools. An enormous wooden pulpit by Antwerp artist Hendrik Verbruggen sees Adam and Eve driven out of Eden by skeletons. To climb the cathedral towers (€5; 10am on the second Saturday of the month), sign up a day or two ahead. (www.cathedralisbruxellensis.be; Place Ste-Gudule; admission free, treasury €1, crypt €3; ⊙7.30am-6pm Mon-Fri, 3.30am-3.30pm Sat, 2-6pm Sun; Ⓜ Gare Centrale)

Manneken Pis MONUMENT

4 ◉ MAP P84, D6

Rue Charles Buls – Brussels' most unashamedly touristy shopping street, lined with chocolate and trinket shops – leads the hordes three blocks from Grand Place to Manneken Pis. This fountain-statue of a little boy taking a leak is comically tiny and a perversely perfect national symbol for surreal Belgium. Most of the time the statue's nakedness is hidden beneath a costume relevant to an anniversary, national day or local event: his ever-growing wardrobe is displayed at the Maison du Roi (p81). (cnr Rue de l'Étuve & Rue du Chêne; Ⓜ Gare Centrale)

Jeanneke Pis   MONUMENT

5 ◉ MAP P84, F4

Squatting just off Rue des Bouchers, this pigtailed female counterpart of Manneken Pis is the work of sculptor Denis Adrien Debouvrie, who installed her here in 1985. She's usually partly obscured by locked iron gates. (Impasse de la Fidélité; Ⓜ Gare Centrale)

Brussels City Museum   MUSEUM

6 ◉ MAP P84, E4

Old maps, architectural relics and paintings give a historical overview of the city. Don't miss

Pieter Brueghel the Elder's 1567 *Cortège de Noces* (Wedding Procession). (Musée de la Ville de Bruxelles; ☏ 02-279 43 50; www. museedelavilledebruxelles.be; Grand Place; adult/concession/BrusselsCard €8/6/free; ◷ 10am-5pm Tue-Sun; Ⓜ Gare Centrale, 🚊 Bourse)

Bruxella 1238   ARCHAEOLOGICAL SITE

7 ◉ MAP P84, D4

Bruxella 1238 is the scanty remains of a Franciscan convent that was bombarded into ruins in 1695. Most of the site is visible by peeping through the glass windows set into the pavement roughly outside Le Cirio *café* (p94). (Rue de la Bourse; €4; ◷ tours in English 10.15am 1st Wed of month; 🚊 Bourse)

Galeries St-Hubert

Mural-Spotting in Brussels

More than 40 comic-strip murals currently enliven alleys and thoroughfares throughout the old city centre, with more added year after year. These bright artworks are a great prompt to explore less-visited neighbourhoods. Some favourites:

Broussaille (Map p84, C5; Rue du Marché au Charbon; 🚌 Bourse) Depicts a young couple arm-in-arm. The original 1991 version showed a couple of very ambiguous sex that the neighbouring gay establishments used to promote the quarter. However, a 1999 repaint seemed to give the black-haired figure a more feminine hairstyle, earrings and (slightly) bigger breasts. Creeping homophobia or honest mistake? Nobody knows.

Cubitus (Map p84, B1; Rue de Flandre; Ⓜ Ste-Catherine) A tetchy-looking Manneken Pis gazes up at his pediment, from which he has been displaced by a grinning, peeing bear.

FC de Kampioenen (Rue du Canal; Ⓜ Ste-Catherine) This bright, dynamic mural features not a football club but a parade of characters based on a TV series that ran from 1990 to 2011. The show was turned into a comic strip by Hec Leemans in 1997.

Josephine Baker (Map p112, B5; Rue des Capucins 9; Ⓜ Porte de Hal) In one of the most distinctive Marolles murals, slinky chanteuse Josephine, with a leopard on a lead, shakes hands with a rotund monk. Behind, both in the mural and in real life, is the looming dome of the Palais de Justice. Baker performed in Brussels in the 1920s and '30s, and famously kept a leopard as a pet.

Peeping Policeman (Map p112, C5; Rue Haute; Ⓜ Louise) This Hergé character uses the terrace end brilliantly for a little spying.

Sacrifice mural (Blvd Barthélémy; Ⓜ Ste-Catherine) In 2016 and 2017 a new series emerged in the city, depicting male and female genitalia and a graphic scene of child sacrifice. The artist is anonymous, and the subject matter is very different from that of the cheerful city-sanctioned murals. Brussels street art just got a whole lot edgier.

Tibet & Duchateau (Map p84, C5; Rue du Bon Secours 9; 🚌 Bourse) Very effectively depicts a life-sized figure teetering towards a trompe l'œil window.

Tintin (Map p84, D5; Rue de l'Étuve; 🚌 Bourse) The most renowned of Belgium's fictional characters.

Église St-Nicolas CHURCH

8 ⊙ MAP P84, D4

Near Bourse, this pint-sized church is as old as Brussels itself. What really makes it notable is its virtual invisibility – the exterior is almost totally encrusted with shops. Appropriately enough, it's dedicated to the patron saint of merchants. (Rue au Beurre 1; ⏰8am-6.30pm Mon-Fri, 9am-6pm Sat, to 7.30pm Sun; 🚇Bourse)

Fondation Jacques Brel MUSEUM

9 ⊙ MAP P84, E6

Chansonnier Jacques Brel (1929–78) made his debut in 1952 at a cabaret in his native Belgium and shot to fame in Paris, where he was a contemporary of Édith Piaf and co, though his songs continued to hark back to the bleak 'flat land' of his native country. At the time of writing, the museum was being redeveloped, with the audio walking tour still available. (📞02-511 10 20; www.jacquesbrel. be; Place de la Vieille Halle aux Blés 11; adult/student €5/3.50, walk with audioguide €8, walk & museum €10; ⏰noon-6pm Tue-Sat, plus Mon Aug; Ⓜ Gare Centrale)

Musée de la Brasserie MUSEUM

10 ⊙ MAP P84, E5

Brussels' brewery museum is authentic in the sense that it occupies the basement of the brewers' guildhall and has some 18th-century brewing equipment. But visitors are often disappointed because it's small and no actual brewing takes place (though you do get a beer at the end). To see a real brewery in action, head to the **Cantillon Brewery** (📞02-520 28 91; www. cantillon.be; Rue Gheude 56; €9.50; ⏰10am-5pm Mon, Tue & Thu-Sat; Ⓜ Clemenceau), which houses the **Musée Bruxellois de la Gueuze**. (📞02-511 49 87; www.beerparadise.be; Grand Place 10; €5; ⏰10am-5pm daily Apr-Nov, from noon Sat & Sun Dec-Mar; Ⓜ Gare Centrale, 🚇Bourse)

Musée du Cacao et du Chocolat MUSEUM

11 ⊙ MAP P84, D5

Exhibits at Brussels' museum of cocoa and chocolate give you a quick rundown of chocolate's history in Europe, along with chocolate's anti-aging and anti-depressant properties. A couple of small treats along the way include a tasting at the praline-making demonstration. Better yet are the museum's occasional one-hour praline-making courses – call for details. (📞02-514 20 48; www. choco-story-brussels.be; Rue de la Tête d'Or 9; adult/concession/under 12yr €6/5/3.40; ⏰10am-4:30pm; Ⓜ Gare Centrale, 🚇Bourse)

Rue des Bouchers STREET

12 ⊙ MAP P84, E4

Uniquely colourful Rue and Petite Rue des Bouchers are a pair of narrow alleys jam-packed with pavement tables, pyramids of lemons and iced displays of fish and crustaceans. It's all gloriously photogenic, but think twice before eating here, as the food standards are generally poor. Don't miss peeping inside marionette theatre Toone (p97) and, nearby, into the wonderful, age-old biscuit shop Dandoy (p92), full of splendid moulds for *speculaas/speculoos* (traditional spiced biscuit) figures. (M De Brouckère)

Eating

Arcadi
BRASSERIE €

13 ⊗ MAP P84, F4

The jars of preserves, beautiful cakes and fruit tarts at this classic and charming bistro entice plenty of Brussels residents, as do well-priced meals such as lasagne and steak, all served nonstop by courteous staff. With a nice location on the edge of the Galeries St-Hubert, this is a great spot for an indulgent, creamy hot chocolate. (☏ 02-511 33 43; www.arcadicafe. be; Rue d'Arenberg 1b; mains €10-15; ⊗ 8am-11.45pm Tue-Fri, from 7.30am Sat, from 9am Sun; M Gare Centrale)

Mer du Nord
SEAFOOD €

14 ⊗ MAP P84, C2

Well-reputed fishmonger's window catering to a wide cross-section of Brussels folk plus assorted visitors – place your order and when it's ready your name is called by staff with a brass megaphone. Eat standing up at tables on the cobbled square opposite. The scampi (not deep fried but soaked in herb dressing) is sublime. (Noordzee; www.vishandelnoordzee.

Mer du Nord

LERNER VADIM/SHUTTERSTOCK ©

be; Rue Ste-Catherine 45; items from €7; ⏱8am-6pm Tue-Fri, to 5pm Sat; MSte-Catherine)

MOK

VEGETARIAN €

15 MAP P84, A1

MOK serves some of the capital's best coffee and offers a wide range of vegan-inspired recipes prepared by Josefien Smets – think crispy tofu and pickled cucumber sandwiches or the legendary avocado toast. A big picture window looks out onto Rue Dansaert. (☏02-513 57 87; www. mokcoffee.be; Rue Antoine Dansaert 196; mains €10-20; ⏱8.30am-6pm Mon-Fri, from 10am Sat & Sun; 🖊; MComte de Flandre)

Cremerie De Linkebeek

DELI €

16 MAP P84, B3

Brussels' best *fromagerie* was established in 1902 and retains its original glazed tiles. It still stocks a beguiling array of cheeses, which you can also try on crunchy baguettes with fresh salad, wrapped in blue-and-white-striped paper ready to take to a nearby bench. (☏02-512 35 10; Rue du Vieux Marché aux Grains 4; items from €5; ⏱9am-3pm Mon, to 6pm Tue-Sat; MSte-Catherine)

Henri

FUSION €€

17 MAP P84, A1

In an airy white space on this street to watch, Henri concocts tangy fusion dishes such as tuna with ginger, soy and lime, arti-

Rue des Bouchers

🍴

Low-hanging awnings strung with fairy lights, oyster stands on the cobblestones and aproned waiters hustling for business cram narrow Rue des Bouchers (p89), which intersects Galeries St-Hubert. Yes, this is tourist central, and due to the generally poor food standards, locals steer clear.

chokes with scampi, lime and olive tapenade, or Argentine fillet steak in parsley. It has an astute wine list and staff who know their stuff. (☏02-218 00 08; www.restohenri. be; Rue de Flandre 113; mains €17-24; ⏱noon-2pm Tue-Fri & 6-10pm Tue-Sat; MSte-Catherine)

Le Cercle des Voyageurs

BRASSERIE €€

18 MAP P84, C6

Delightful bistro featuring globes, an antique-map ceiling and a travel library. If your date's late, flick through an old *National Geographic* in your colonial leather chair. The global brasserie food is pretty good, and there are documentary screenings and free live music: piano jazz on Tuesday and experimental on Thursday. Other gigs in the cave have a small entrance fee. (☏02-514 39 49; www.lecercledesvoyageurs.com; Rue des Grands Carmes 18; mains €15-21; ⏱11am-midnight; 🖊; 🚊Bourse, Anneessens)

Waffling on about Waffles

Locals get 'real' waffles at **Mokafé** (Map p84, F4; 02-511 78 70; Galerie du Roi; waffles from €3; 7.30am-11.30pm; De Brouckère), an old-fashioned cafe under the glass arch of the Galeries St-Hubert (p86). It's a little timeworn inside, but wicker chairs in the beautiful arcade provide you with a good view of passing shoppers. Note that traditional waffles have 20 squares, and are dusted with icing sugar rather than loaded with cream.

L'Ogenblik FRENCH €€€

19 MAP P84, F4

It may be only a stone's throw from Rue des Bouchers, but this timeless bistro with its lace curtains, resident cat, marble-topped tables and magnificent wrought-iron lamp feels a world away. It has been producing French classics for more than 30 years, and the expertise shows. Worth the price for a special meal in the heart of town. (02-511 61 51; www.ogenblik.be; Galerie des Princes 1; mains €25-33; noon-2.30pm & 6.30pm-midnight Mon-Sat; Bourse)

Nona PIZZA €

20 MAP P84, C3

With a striped monochrome awning, marbled counter and Neapolitan slow-rising-dough pizzas, Nona is a slice of *bella vita* in Brussels. Barring Italian tomatoes and olive oil, the ingredients are Belgian and mostly organic, including the *mozzarella di bufala*. Try wintry pizzas featuring pumpkin and bacon, or gorgonzola, pear and pine nuts, or perhaps the vegetarian 'From Dries with Love'. (02-324 78 79; www.nonalife.com; Rue Ste-Catherine 17-19; pizzas €7-14; noon-10pm Sun-Wed, to 11pm Thu-Sat; Ste-Catherine)

Dandoy BAKERY €

21 MAP P84, D4

Established in 1829, Brussels' best-known *biscuiterie* has five local branches, this one with an attached tearoom. The chocolate for Dandoy's choc-dipped biscuits is handmade by Laurent Gerbaud. (02-511 03 26; www.maisondandoy.com; Rue au Beurre 31; snacks from €6; 9.30am-7pm Mon-Sat, from 10.30am Sun; Bourse)

Charli BAKERY €

22 MAP P84, C3

A fabulous little bakery housed in a gabled building whose cute frontage is painted with a colourful map. There's posh patisserie fodder, as well as croissants and *pain au chocolat* for a bargain €1.50. Ingredients are organic and natural, and everything is made in-house. A great spot for a sweet treat after fishy takeout at nearby Mer du Nord (p90). (02-513 63 32; www.charliboulangerie.com; Rue Ste-Catherine 34; items from €1.50;

⊙7.30am-7pm Mon-Sat, 8am-1.30pm Sun; Ⓜ️Ste-Catherine)

Chez Léon
BELGIAN €€

23 ❌ MAP P84, F4

This long-time tourist favourite serves the original 'Mussels from Brussels', and makes a good place to try them if you don't mind that portions (mostly 850g) are somewhat small by Belgian standards. Rooms are spread over several gabled houses and decor varies from attractively classic to somewhat tacky, depending on where you sit. (📞02-513 04 26; www.chezleon.be; Rue des Bouchers 18; mains €15-27; ⊙11.30am-11pm; Ⓜ️Gare Centrale)

In 't Spinnekopke
BELGIAN €€

24 ❌ MAP P84, A4

This age-old classic occupies an atmospheric 17th-century white-washed cottage, with a summer terrace spilling onto the revamped square. Bruxellois specialities and meats cooked in beer-based sauces are authentic but hardly a bargain, and some of the tables feel a tad cramped. (📞02-511 86 95; www.spinnekopke.be; Place du Jardin aux Fleurs 1; mains €15-25; ⊙noon-2.30pm & 7-10.30pm Mon-Fri, 7-10.30pm Sat; 🚊Bourse)

Bij den Boer
SEAFOOD €€

25 ❌ MAP P84, B1

Convivial fish restaurant, with mirror-panelled walls, model yachts, sensible prices and a jolly ambience. The wine of the month is €20 a bottle. (📞02-512 61 22; www.bijdenboer.com; Quai aux Briques 60; mains €15-28, menu €29.50; ⊙noon-2.30pm & 6-10.30pm Mon-Sat; Ⓜ️Ste-Catherine)

Drinking

Goupil le Fol
BAR

26 🍺 MAP P84, E6

Overwhelming weirdness hits you as you acid-trip your way through this sensory overload of rambling passageways, ragged old sofas and inexplicable beverages mostly based on madly fruit-flavoured wines (no beer is served). Un-missable. (📞02-511 13 96; www.goupillefol.com; Rue de la Violette 22; ⊙4pm-2am; Ⓜ️Gare Centrale)

A l'Imaige de Nostre-Dame
PUB

27 🍺 MAP P84, E4

Down a tiny hidden alley from Rue du Marché aux Herbes 5, Nostre-Dame has an almost medieval feel but retains a genuine local vibe. A magical old café...except for the toilets. (Rue du Marché aux Herbes 8; ⊙noon-midnight Mon-Fri, 3pm-1am Sat, 4-10.30pm Sun; 🚊Bourse)

Toone
BAR

28 🍺 MAP P84, E4

At the home to Brussels' classic puppet theatre (p97), this irresisti-bly quaint and cosy timber-framed bar serves beers and basic snacks. (Petite Rue des Bouchers; beer from

€2.50; ⏰noon-midnight Tue-Sun; Ⓜ Gare Centrale)

Le Cirio   PUB

29 🚌 MAP P84, D4

This sumptuous 1886 *grand café* dazzles with polished brasswork and aproned waiters, yet prices aren't exorbitant and coiffured *mesdames* with small dogs still dilute the gaggles of tourists. The house speciality is a half-and-half mix of still and sparkling wines. (📞02-512 13 95; Rue de la Bourse 18; ⏰10am-midnight; 🚊Bourse)

Monk   BAR

30 🚌 MAP P84, B2

Dark wood, a piano and opal lights set the mood of this classic Belgian pub. Mostly attended by Flemish locals, Monk serves a wide array of reasonably priced draught and bottled beers. (📞02-511 75 11; www.monk.be; Rue Ste-Catherine 42; ⏰11am-2am Mon-Sat, from 2pm Sun; Ⓜ Ste-Catherine)

Via Via Café   BAR

31 🚌 MAP P84, B1

Rub shoulders with a Flemish crowd at this industrial *café*, with brick and concrete floors, away from the nearby touristy hot spots. Try local beers such as those from Brussels Beer Project, or a homemade soft. The large open bar room is stocked with boardgames and guidebooks, and there's another bar and events space upstairs. (www.viavia.world/en/belgium/brussels; Quai aux Briques 74; ⏰3pm-midnight Mon, to 1am Tue-Thu, to 2.30am Fri, 2pm-2.30am Sat, to midnight Sun; Ⓜ Ste-Catherine)

Brussels Beer Project   BREWERY

32 🚌 MAP P84, A1

With sumptuous beers and a constant flow of new brews taste-tested by the public, this democratic microbrewery and bar is one of the most innovative players in Brussels' beer scene. Classic BPP brews like the Delta IPA and Grosse Bertha wheat beer are on sale in the taproom, with brewery tours available too. (📞02-502 28 56; www.beerproject.be; Rue Antoine Dansaert 188; ⏰2-10pm Thu-Sat; 🚊51)

BarBeton   BAR

33 🚌 MAP P84, A1

Typical of the new array of hip but relaxed Brussels bars, BarBeton has a tiled floor and unpolished wood furnishings. It's good for an early breakfast, and there's a lavish €15 brunch on Sunday. Cocktail happy hour is 7pm to 8pm Thursday, there's an *aperitivo* buffet from 6pm to 8pm Friday, and DJs play from 10pm till late on Saturday. (📞02-513 83 63; www.barbeton.be; Rue Antoine Dansaert 114; ⏰10am-midnight; 📶; Ⓜ Ste-Catherine)

Au Bon Vieux Temps   PUB

34 🚌 MAP P84, E4

Duck beneath the statue of the bishop, then tunnel through the centuries to this panelled 1695 gem.

You'll find lavish fireplaces, fascinating characters and even legendary Westvleteren 12 on the beer menu. (📞02-217 26 26; Impasse St-Nicolas; ⏰11am-midnight; 🚋Bourse)

Poechenellekelder PUB

35 🚇 MAP P84, D6

Despite facing Brussels' kitsch central, this is a surprisingly appealing *café* full of genuine old puppets. It offers a great selection of fairly priced beers, including Oerbier and *gueuze* (a type of lambic beer) on tap. (Rue du Chêne 5; ⏰11am-1am Tue-Sun; 🚋Bruxelles Central)

La Fleur en Papier Doré PUB

36 🚇 MAP P84, C6

The nicotine-stained walls of this tiny *café*, adored by artists and locals, are covered with writings, art and scribbles by Magritte and his surrealist pals, some of which were reputedly traded for free drinks. *'Ceci n'est pas un musée'* ('This is not a museum') quips a sign on the door reminding visitors to buy a drink and not just look around. (📞02-511 16 59; www.goudblommeke inpapier.be; Rue des Alexiens 53; ⏰11am-midnight Tue-Sat, to 7pm Sun; 🚋Bruxelles Central)

Walvis BAR

37 🚇 MAP P84, A1

Sounds from soul to punk to progressive rock (live, DJs or just through the speakers) play at this ubercool bar, where entry's free, the atmosphere buzzes and the staff are great. (📞02-219 95 32; www.cafewalvis.be; Rue Antoine

Le Cirio

Dansaert; ⏰11am-2am Mon-Thu & Sun, to 4am Fri & Sat; 📶; Ⓜ Ste-Catherine)

À la Mort Subite
BROWN CAFE

38 🚇 MAP P84, G3

An absolute classic unchanged since 1928, with lined-up wooden tables, arched mirror panels and entertainingly brusque service. (📞02-513 13 18; www.alamortsubite.com; Rue Montagne aux Herbes Potagères 7; ⏰11am-1am Mon-Sat, noon-midnight Sun; Ⓜ Gare Centrale)

Bar des Amis
BAR

39 🚇 MAP P84, C3

A great bar to kick-start a night out, right in the centre of the vibrant Ste-Catherine area. The cosy atmosphere is enhanced by vintage items hanging on the walls. A separate smoking room inside the bar is good news for smokers, especially on cold days. (www.bardesamis.be; Rue Ste-Catherine 30; ⏰5pm-late Sun-Thu, from 3pm Fri & Sat; 📶; Ⓜ Ste-Catherine)

Métropole Café
CAFE

40 🚇 MAP P84, E2

The magnificently ornate belle époque interior easily justifies the hefty drink prices, though, curiously, a large number of punters still decide to sit on its comparatively unappealing street terrace. (Hotel Métropole; www.metropolehotel.com; Place de Brouckère 31; beer/coffee/waffles from €4/4/8; 📶; Ⓜ De Brouckère)

Le Belgica
BAR

41 🚇 MAP P84, D5

DJs transform what looks like a traditional 1920s' brown *café* into one of Brussels' most popular gay music pubs. (www.lebelgica.be; Rue du Marché au Charbon 32; ⏰10pm-3am Thu-Sun; 🚇Bourse)

Entertainment

L'Archiduc
JAZZ

42 ⭐ MAP P84, C3

This intimate, split-level art deco bar has been playing jazz since 1937. It's an unusual, two-tiered circular space that can get incredibly packed but remains convivial. You might need to ring the doorbell to get in. Saturday concerts (5pm) are free; Sunday brings in international talent and admission charges vary. (📞02-512 0652; www.archiduc.net; Rue Antoine Dansaert 6; ⏰4pm-5am; 🚇Bourse)

Cinéma Galeries
CINEMA

43 ⭐ MAP P84, F4

Inside the graceful, glassed-over Galeries St-Hubert, this art deco beauty concentrates on foreign and art-house films. An authentic Brussels movie experience. (📞02-514 74 98; www.arenberg.be; Galerie de la Reine 26; 🚇Bourse)

Music Village
JAZZ

44 ⭐ MAP P84, D4

A polished 100-seat jazz venue housed in two 17th-century buildings with dinner (not compulsory) available from 7pm and concerts starting at 8.30pm or 9pm at weekends. The performers squeeze onto a small podium that's visible from any seat. Bookings advised. (📞02-513 13 45; www.themusicvillage.com; Rue des Pierres 50; cover €7.50-20; ⏰from 7.30pm Wed-Sat; 🚇Bourse)

Théâtre Royal de Toone
THEATRE

45 ⭐ MAP P84, E4

Eight generations of the Toone family have staged classic puppet productions in the Bruxellois dialect at this endearing marionette theatre, a highlight of any visit to Brussels. Shows are aimed at adults, but kids love them too. (📞02-511 71 37; www.toone.be; Petite Rue des Bouchers 21; adult/child

€10/7; ⏰typically 8.30pm Thu & 4pm Sat; 🚇Gare Centrale)

Cabaret Mademoiselle
CABARET

46 ⭐ MAP P84, C5

Burlesque and brassy, Cabaret Mademoiselle is a new venue that combines drag, circus and comedy, served up with some first-rate Belgian beers. (📞0474 58 57 61; www.cabaretmademoiselle.be; Rue du Marché au Charbon 53; admission free; ⏰7pm-late Wed-Sat; 🚇Bourse)

Art Base
LIVE MUSIC

47 ⭐ MAP P84, H2

One of the best little venues in town for music fans with eclectic tastes. It resembles someone's living room, but the programming is first rate, and it's worth taking

Brussels Grand Place & Îlot Sacré

Posters in Théâtre Royal de Toone

Jazz in Brussels

Jazz has a special place in Belgium, the home of Adolphe Sax (inventor of the saxophone), Romany guitar king Django Reinhardt and harmonica whiz Toots Thielemans. Along with Music Village (p96), long established and much-loved venues include the **Jazz Station** (📞02-733 13 78; www.jazzstation.be; Chaussée de Louvain 193a; ⏰exhibitions 11am-7pm Wed-Sat, concerts 6pm Sat & 8.30pm some weeknights; Ⓜ️Madou), L'Archiduc (p96) and **Sounds** (📞02-512 92 50; www.soundsjazzclub.be; Rue de la Tulipe 28; ⏰8pm-4am Mon-Sat; Ⓜ️Porte de Namur) in Ixelles. The Brussels Jazz Weekend (www.brusselsjazzweekend.be) is held in venues across the city in May.

a punt on Greek *rebetiko,* Indian classical music, chamber concerts, Argentine guitar or whatever else is playing. (📞02-217 29 20; www.art-base.be; Rue des Sables 29; ⏰Fri & Sat; Ⓜ️Rogier)

Bizon
BLUES

48 ⭐ MAP P84, C3

A happening little grunge bar in St-Géry featuring home-grown live blues, a range of beers and a selection of *jenevers* (gin). Located on a street of lively *café*-bars. (📞02-502 46 99; www.cafebizon.com; Rue du Pont de la Carpe 7; ⏰4pm-late, from 6pm Sat & Sun; 🚇Bourse)

Palace Cinema
CINEMA

49 ⭐ MAP P84, C4

An impressive 1905 picture palace and music hall reinvented: this is the city's oldest cinema, housed in a fine art nouveau building. For part of its history the place was a nightclub. The angular lobby incorporates rough-hewn concrete pillars and a ceiling hung with wacky lamps, while the four screens show a mixture of art-house and mainstream movies. (📞02-503 57 96; www.cinema-palace.be; Blvd Anspach 85; €8.75; 🚇Bourse)

Chez Maman
CABARET

50 ⭐ MAP P84, C6

Chez Maman features the capital's most beloved transvestite show: Maman has been wowing the crowds here for over 20 years. (📞02-502 86 96; www.chezmaman.be; Rue des Grands Carmes 12; ⏰from 10pm Fri & Sat; 🚇Anneessens)

Shopping

Gabriele
VINTAGE

51 🔒 MAP P84, B3

For amazing vintage finds, try eccentric, elegant Gabriele. There's a gorgeous jumble of cocktail dresses, hats, Chinese shawls and accessories; only original clothes from the '20s to the '80s are stocked. (📞02-512 67 43; www.gabrielevintage.com; Rue des Chartreux 27; 🕐1-7pm Mon & Tue, from 11am Wed-Sat; 🚇Bourse)

Passa Porta
BOOKS

52 🏠 MAP P84, B3

This stylish bookshop located down an alley has a small but classy English-language section. Check the website for forthcoming literary events, many of which are hosted in English. In the spirit of Victor Hugo, the bookshop supports a writer-in-residence program, and assists in housing exiled authors. (www.passaporta.be; Rue Antoine Dansaert 46; 🕐11am-7pm Tue-Sat, noon-6pm Sun; 🚇Bourse)

Mary
CHOCOLATE

53 🏠 MAP P84, H4

Supplies artisan pralines to Belgium's royals plus the occasional US president. (📞02-217 45 00; www.mary.be; Rue Royale 73; chocolate per kg €58; 🕐10am-6pm Mon-Sat; MMadou)

Planète Chocolat
CHOCOLATE

54 🏠 MAP P84, D5

Both moulds and chocolates are made on-site. At 4pm on Saturday and Sunday there are praline-making demonstrations explaining chocolate's development, culminating in a chance for visitors to create their own chocolates. (📞02-511 07 55; www.planetechocolat.be; Rue du Lombard 24; chocolate per kg €50; 🕐11am-6pm Mon & Sun, 10.30am-6.30pm Tue-Sat; 🚇Bourse)

Chocolates at Mary

Brussels Grand Place & îlot Sacré

Neuhaus

CHOCOLATE

55 🔒 MAP P84, F4

Belgium's original – established in 1857. This stunning flagship shop has stained-glass windows and sumptuous displays. It is the home of the praline, invented here in 1912. (📞02-512 63 59; www.neuhaus. be; Galerie de la Reine 25; chocolate per kg €52; ⏱10am-8pm Mon-Sat, to 7pm Sun; Ⓜ Gare Centrale)

De Biertempel

DRINKS

56 🔒 MAP P84, E4

As its name states, this shop is a temple to beer, stocking upwards of 700 brews along with matching glasses and other booze-related merchandise. For more ordinary beers and for bulk purchases, do like the locals do and go to the supermarket. (📞02-502 19 06; http://biertempel.wixsite.com/debier tempel; Rue du Marché aux Herbes 56b; ⏱9.30am-7pm; 🚇Bourse)

Boutique Tintin

BOOKS

57 🔒 MAP P84, E5

No prizes for guessing the star of this comic shop, which stocks albums galore and cute merchandise. (📞02-514 51 52; http://en.tintin. com; Rue de la Colline 13; ⏱10am-6pm Mon-Sat, 11am-5pm Sun; 👫; Ⓜ Gare Centrale)

Sterling Books

BOOKS

58 🔒 MAP P84, F2

English-language bookshop with comfy sofas and a kids' play area. (📞02-223 62 23; www.sterlingbooks. be; Rue du Fossé aux Loups 23;

De Biertempel

10am-7pm Mon-Sat, noon-6.30pm Sun; M De Brouckère)

Tropismes BOOKS

59 🔒 MAP P84, F4

With its gold-wreath-encircled columns and ornate gilded ceiling, this is about the prettiest bookshop you could imagine. The literary connections are hot too: this is where the exiled Victor Hugo visited his lover/assistant Juliette Drouet. Some titles are in English. (🕿 02-512 88 52; http://tropismes. com; Galerie des Princes 11; ⏱11am-6.30pm Mon, 10am-6.30pm Tue-Thu, 10am-7.30pm Fri, 10.30am-7pm Sat, 1.30-6.30pm Sun; M Gare Centrale)

Martin Margiela FASHION & ACCESSORIES

60 🔒 MAP P84, B1

Margiela is often tagged the unofficial seventh member of a group of designers known as the Antwerp Six (he graduated from Antwerp's fashion academy in 1980). Shoes, accessories and men's and women's body-skimming fashions in understated colours are artfully arranged in this white-on-white boutique. (www.maisonmargiela.com; Rue de Flandre 114; ⏱11am-7pm Mon-Sat; M Ste-Catherine)

Stijl FASHION & ACCESSORIES

61 🔒 MAP P84, B2

A top address, Stijl is well stocked with Antwerp Six classic designer ware (Ann Demeulemeester, Dries Van Noten) but also features up-to-the-minute designers, including Haider Ackermann, Gustavo Lins and Raf Simons. It's a hip place but not unduly daunting to enter, and unlike many such boutiques, prices are clearly labelled. Has fashion for men and women. (🕿 02-512 03 13; www.stijl.be; Rue Antoine Dansaert 74; ⏱10.30am-6.30pm Mon-Sat; M Ste-Catherine)

Walking Tour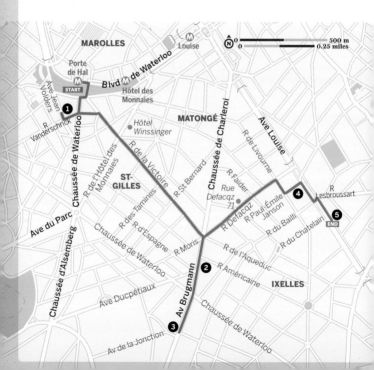

Art Nouveau Brussels

Art nouveau is the signature architectural style of Brussels. Its most significant exponent was Victor Horta (1861–1947), who's mostly remembered for daring, light-suffused buildings constructed with wrought iron and glass. Some of his surviving masterpieces can be explored on this route, along with lovely buildings by his contemporaries.

Walking Facts

Start Porte de Hal
End Ave Louise
Length 3.5km; two hours

❶ La Porteuse d'Eau

Head down Chaussée de Waterloo from the fairy-tale Porte de Hal, and turn right onto Ave Jean Volders. At No 48 you can have a coffee at classic art nouveau La Porteuse d'Eau, featuring spectacular stained glass and ornate wooden booths. The Hôtel Winssinger, at Rue de l'Hôtel des Monnaies 66, is a typically sober, unostentatious Horta building. Look for the characteristic pale stone, as well as the use of metal around the windows and the dainty swirling balconies.

❷ Musée Horta

You may want to visit Musée Horta (p138) separately to give yourself plenty of time here. But do pause to admire the exterior, characteristically simple but featuring a playful motif on the dragonfly terrace.

❸ Les Hiboux & Hôtel Hannon

Ave Brugmann brings you to two delightful adjoining art nouveau buildings: Édouard Pelseneer's red-brick **Les Hiboux** (Ave Brugmann 55), surmounted by two Gothic owls, and Jules Brunfaut's **Hôtel Hannon** (Ave de la Jonction 1), graced by stone friezes and stained glass. Furth south, at Ave Brugmann 80, is another Horta building, commissioned by his friend, designer Fernand Dubois. It's now the Cuban embassy, but you can see from the outside how the large windows must have flooded the studio with light.

❹ Hôtel Tassel

Paul Hankar's buildings on Rue Defacqz are externally much more exuberant constructs than Horta's. **Rue Defacqz 71** is an 1893 house designed by Hankar (1859–1901) as his own studio. Rue Paul-Émile Janson 6 is the site of Horta's first truly art nouveau house, the 1893 **Hôtel Tassel**. Horta designed the mosaics, stained glass, woodwork and even the door handles.

❺ Hôtel Solvay

At No 224 on grandiose Ave Louise you'll find Horta-designed Hôtel Solvay, also considered one of his masterpieces. Again, he designed every element of the house, incorporating luxurious materials such as tropical wood, bronze and onyx. It's open only to ARAU tours (p22).

Walking Tour 🚶

Shopping in Ste-Catherine

Ste-Catherine is a byword for what's hippest and happening fashion-wise in the capital. The main drag, Rue Antoine Dansaert, forms the focal point for Brussels' fashion scene, featuring avant garde home-grown designers, while Rue de Flandre and Rue Léon Lepage host smaller and quirkier boutiques. Window shop or drop some cash, and hang out in the hip neighbourhood cafés (pubs).

Walking Facts
Start Gabriele
End Wonderloop
Length 850m

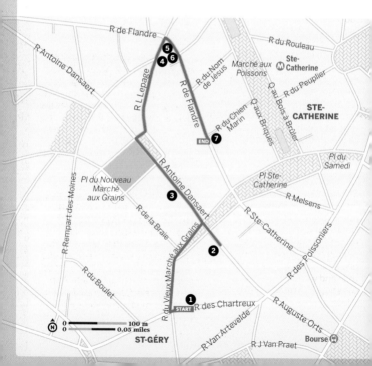

❶ Gabriele

Venerable Gabriele (p98) near the Bourse is the ultimate vintage treasure trove in Brussels – and there's a lot of competition. Some of the garments are collector's items: you'll find men's trilbies and spats, parasols, costume jewels dripping with fake stones, evening dresses and much more. A great spot to grab some garb for a night at the art deco L'Archiduc jazz club nearby.

❷ Passa Porta

Tucked down a passageway, the lovely Passa Porta (p99) bookshop is well worth a look, particularly as it has a strong, very literary focussed English-language selection. If you're looking to make friends and contacts in Brussels, it's a great first stop, as there are regular literary events. Passa Porta support and host writers in exile, such as Moroccan journalist Ali Amar.

❸ Stijl

Stijl (p101) is the showcase for long-established but still edgy Antwerp designers such as Ann Demeulemeester and Dries Van Noten. The picture windows display covetable asymmetrical and beautifully cut garments for men and women. Don't be shy – the shop is more welcoming than it looks.

❹ Just in Case

Floating and feminine garments with vintage-style shapes. The beautiful women's clothes at **Just in Case** (www.justincase.be; Rue Léon Lepage 63; ⊙11am-7pm Tue-Sat) feature bold stripes and bird-of-paradise prints.

❺ Au Laboureur

Sample old Brussels when you need some refreshment: characterful corner bar **Au Laboureur** (Rue de Flandre 108; beer €1.60; ⊙9.30am-10pm) is a great beer-stop and a reminder of the area's past.

❻ Oxfam

As befits this area, the colourful, vibrant **Oxfam** (☑02-522 40 70; Rue de Flandre 104; ⊙11am-6pm Mon-Sat) secondhand clothes store is a cut above, with some gorgeous jackets, day dresses and blouses arrayed in rainbow colours. Costume jewels and accessories too, all at bargain prices. There's also a small men's section.

❼ Wonderloop

New eco and Fairtrade clothing store **Wonderloop** (www.wonderloop.be; Rue de Flandre 35; ⊙11am-7pm Tue-Sat), for men and women, is a welcome addition to the scene. Check out the colourful Pan Africa sneakers, made from bright African fabrics in Casablanca. Many of the garments are handmade in Belgium.

Explore ◈
Royal Quarter

The majestic Royal Quarter takes in the Palais Royal, the grandiose Palais de Justice, and the Mont des Arts, where Brussels' premier museums are housed in some of the city's most magnificent buildings, all just a few steps from each other. Antique shops, tearooms and chocolate boutiques cluster around the Place du Grand Sablon, while graceful churches and the elegant Parc de Bruxelles add to the area's rarefied air.

A day of cultural appreciation begins at the Musées Royaux des Beaux-Arts (p108) and the adjoining Musée Magritte (p109). Head to one of the cafes on the Place du Grand Sablon for lunch, or pick up a picnic at Claire Fontaine (p117) and enjoy it in the Place du Petit Sablon (p115) in the shadow of Église Notre-Dame du Sablon (p114). In the afternoon, marvel at Brussels' musical-instrument museum, MIM (p110) or, to find out more about Belgium's history, check out the Musée BELvue (p116). For dinner enjoy brasserie food at Le Perroquet (p118), or book ahead for fine dining at Les Brigittines (p118), followed by a silent movie with live piano accompaniment at Cinematek (p120).

Getting There & Around

Ⓜ Louise and Porte de Namur are the handiest for the Place du Sablon; Gare Central is best for Mont des Arts.

🚋 Numbers 92, 93 and 94 all pass through the district.

Neighbourhood Map on p112

Park on Mont des Arts S-F/SHUTTERSTOCK ©

Top Sight 📷

Musées Royaux des Beaux-Arts

The prestigious Royal Museums of Fine Arts incorporates the **Musée d'Art Ancien** (ancient art) in which the 15th-century Flemish Primitives are wonderfully represented; the **Musée d'Art Moderne** (modern art), with works by surrealist Paul Delvaux and fauvist Rik Wouters, among others; and the purpose-built **Musée Magritte**, which houses the world's largest collection of the surrealist pioneer's paintings and drawings.

◎ MAP P112, E3

📞 02-508 32 11

www.fine-arts-museum.be

Rue de la Régence 3

adult/6-25yr/Brussels-Card €10/3/free, incl Magritte Museum €15

🕙 10am-5pm Tue-Fri, 11am-6pm Sat & Sun

Ⓜ Gare Centrale, Parc

Flemish Primitives

The work of these 15th-century masters is wonderfully represented in the gallery: look out for Roger Van der Weyden's *Pietà* with its strange dawn sky; Dieric Bouts' dramatic tableau depicting the torments of an unjustly accused husband and his faithful wife in *Justice of the Emperor Otto*, and the delicate *Madonna with Saints* by the anonymous artist known as the Master of the Legend of St Lucy.

The Brueghels

While Pieter the Elder was the greatest of this family of artists, his sons' work echoed his humorous and tender scenes, where the central narrative of the painting often has to be sought out among a wealth of lively rustic detail. The most famous example is the *Fall of Icarus*, where the hero's legs disappearing into the waves are overshadowed by the figure of an unconcerned ploughman and a jaunty ship.

Rubens & His Followers

Antwerp painter Pieter Paul Rubens specialised in fleshy religious works, of which there are several colossal examples here. But his lesser-known works, such as his *Studies of a Negro's Head* show he was also a master of psychological portraiture. In this section, look out too for Anthony Van Dyck's contemplative human studies, Cornelius De Vos' charming family portrait, and works by Rembrandt and Frans Hals.

Musée Magritte

This adjoining **museum** (☏02-508 32 11; www.musee-magritte-museum.be; Place Royale 1; adult/under 26yr/BrusselsCard €10/3/free; ☉10am-5pm Tue-Fri, 11am-6pm Sat & Sun) offers a chronological exploration of the artist's work, including surreal and playful photos and films. In his famous canvases, motifs of spheres, pipes and birds appear repeatedly, as does the image of his wife Georgette.

★ Top Tips

○ Consider visiting Musée Magritte separately, as it merits at least two hours. You can buy a joint ticket and return another day.

○ The museum also hosts acclaimed temporary exhibitions, for which there's an extra charge.

○ Check out the small sculpture garden, to the left as you face the building.

✗ Take a Break

The museum cafe is a pricey but pleasant spot serving sandwiches, salads and cakes, with a terrace punctuated with statues overlooking the rooftops.

Claire Fontaine (p117) nearby has homemade food to go.

Top Sight 📷
MIM

Strap on a pair of headphones at the Musée des Instruments de Musique, then step on the automated floor panels in front of the precious instruments (including world instruments and Adolphe Sax's inventions) to hear them being played. As much of a highlight is the premises itself – the art nouveau Old England Building.

◎ MAP P112, F3

☎ 02-545 01 30

www.mim.be

Rue Montagne de la Cour 2

adult/concession €10/8

🕓 9.30am-5pm Tue-Fri, from 10am Sat & Sun

Ⓜ Gare Centrale, Parc

Sound Lab

The exhibits in this dimly lit gallery are numbered, with each number corresponding to a point on the soundtrack you hear via headphones. Sounds range from a 16th-century church bell chiming midnight to a 19th-century bird organ and 20th-century Hammond organ blues. Among the artefacts is a barrel organ with wooden figures that, when animated, enact various grisly teeth-pulling operations.

Traditional Instruments

This gallery contains every instrument you've ever heard of, and then some. You can appreciate the aesthetic qualities of actual instruments from around the world as well as – via the headphones – musical mastery, from the intricacies of the Indian sitar to the otherworldly wail of Tibetan horns to Congolese drums and harps. One of the weirdest sights and sounds is the Mardi Gras bear mask from Limbourg in Belgium, sitting alongside rough-hewn instruments and with accompanying primitive chants.

Western Art Music

A precious collection of Western wind, string and keyboard instruments. The early variations on pianos, painted with delicate flowers and pastoral scenes, are among the most attractive items on display; look out too for the huge serpent-headed bassoons. As with the other galleries, plug in your headphones to listen as well as look.

Old England Building

The art nouveau Old England Building is as much of a highlight as the museum itself. This former department store was built in 1899 by Paul Saintenoy and has a panoramic rooftop cafe and terrace.

★ Top Tips

○ Headphones are essential for a visit, but don't worry if you don't speak French or Dutch – all you'll hear is music.

○ There is no labelling in English, so collect a handout at the entrance to each gallery.

○ To see the building but not the museum, take the lift to the top floor and make your way back down via the stairs.

○ There are regular concerts in the museum's recital hall, some of them free; check the What's On section of the website.

✕ Take a Break

Head to the top floor for spectacular views framed by wrought-iron curlicues at **Cafetéria du MIM** (📞 02-502 95 08; www.mim.be/the-restaurant; meals €12-16; ⏰ 10am-4.30pm, closed Mon).

Or head a little downhill to sample sugar-free chocs at Laurent Gerbaud (p117).

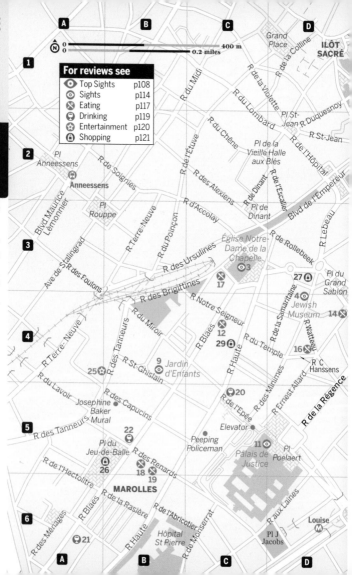

For reviews see

◉ Top Sights	p108
◎ Sights	p114
✖ Eating	p117
✖ Drinking	p119
★ Entertainment	p120
🏠 Shopping	p121

0
0
400 m
0.2 miles

Grand Place

ILÔT SACRÉ

R de la Colline

R de la Violette

R du Midi

R du Lombard

R du Chêne

Pl St-Jean

R Duquesnoy

R St-Jean

R de l'Hôpital

Pl de la Vieille Halle aux Blés

R de l'Étuve

R des Alexiens

R de Dinant

R de l'Escalier

Blvd de l'Empereur

R d'Accolay

Pl de Dinant

R de Rollebeek

R de Soignies

Pl Anneessens

Anneessens

Pl Rouppe

R Terre-Neuve

R du Poinçon

Blvd Maurice Lemonnier

Ave de Stalingrad

R des Foulons

R des Ursulines

Église Notre-Dame de la Chapelle ◎3

R de la Samaritaine

Jewish Museum

Pl du Grand Sablon

R Lebeau

27🏠

4◎

14🏠

R Watteau

16🏠

R des Brigittines

✖17

R Notre Seigneur

R Blaes

12◎

29🏠

R du Temple

R Haute

R des Minimes

R Ernest Allard

R C Hanssens

R Terre-Neuve

R du Miroir

R des Tanneurs

R St-Ghislain

9 Jardin d'Enfants

◎20

R de l'Épée

R de la Régence

R du Lavoir

25✖

R des Capucins

Josephine Baker Mural

Elevator

22🏠

Pl du Jeu-de-Balle

26🏠

R des Renards

18✖ 19✖

Peeping Policeman

11◉

Pl Poelaert

Palais de Justice

R des Tanneurs

R de l'Hectolitre

MAROLLES

R Blaes

R de la Rasière

R de l'Abricotier

R aux Laines

◎21

R des Ménages

R Haute

Hôpital St Pierre

R de Monserrat

Pl J Jacobs

Louise Ⓜ

E

Carr de l'Impératrice

Blvd de l'Impératrice

Carr de l'Europe

F

Ⓜ Gare Centrale

R Ravenstein

G

Palais de la Nation

R de la Loi

Ⓜ Parc

Théâtre du Parc

H

1

Ⓜ Bruxelles-Central

Pl de l'Albertine

Mont des Arts

5 ◉ Bibliothèque Royale

R Royale

13 ⊗

R Baron Horta

23 ✪ 24 ✪

2 ◉ Parc de Bruxelles

R Ducale

2

SABLON

R Montagne de la Cour

MIM ◉

Musée Magritte

Pl Royale

BIP ℹ

Coudenberg

10 ◉ 8 ◉ Musée BELvue

Pl des Palais

Ave des Arts

3

Musées Royaux des Beaux-Arts ◉

R de la Régence

R Villa Hermosa

7 ◉ Palais Royal

Parc de Bruxelles

Trône Ⓜ

Pl du Trône

R du Trône

🔒 28

1 ◉ Église Notre-Dame du Sablon

R Bréderode

UPPER TOWN

4

6 ◉ Place du Petit Sablon

ROYAL QUARTER

R de Namur

Porte de Namur Ⓜ

MATONGÉ

R du Champ de Mars

Pl du Champ de Mars

R aux Laines

Parc d'Egmont

15 ⊗

Blvd de Waterloo

Ave de la Toison d'Or

Square du Bastion

R de Stassart

Chaussée de Wavre

R d'Edimbourg

MATONGÉ

5

Pl Louise

R Cap Crespel

R des Draplers

R des Chevallers

R du Berger

R Keyenveld

Chaussée d'Ixelles

R.E. Solvay

R Longue Vie

R de la Paix

6

E   **F**   **G**   **H**

Sights

Église Notre-Dame du Sablon

CHURCH

1  MAP P112, E4

The Sablon's large, flamboyantly Gothic church started life as the 1304 archers' guild chapel. A century later it had to be massively enlarged to cope with droves of pilgrims attracted by the supposed healing powers of its Madonna statue. The statue was procured in 1348 by means of an audacious theft from an Antwerp church – apparently by a vision-motivated husband-and-wife team in a rowing boat. It has long since gone, but a boat behind the pulpit commemorates the curious affair. (Rue de la Régence; 9am-6.30pm Mon-Fri, from 10am Sat & Sun; M Porte de Namur)

Parc de Bruxelles

PARK

2  MAP P112, G2

Brussels is well endowed with outlying forests and parklands, but in the inner city it's a different story. The largest central patch of greenery is Parc de Bruxelles, an old, formal park flanked by the Palais Royal and the Palais de la Nation. Laid out under the auspices of the dukes of Brabant, it's dotted with classical statues and framed by trees with mercilessly trellised branches. Lunchtime office workers, joggers and families with kids love it in summer. (Pl des Palais; M Parc, 92, 93 or 94)

Église Notre-Dame du Sablon

SERGEY DZYUBA/SHUTTERSTOCK ©

Église Notre-Dame de la Chapelle   CHURCH

3 ⊙ MAP P112, C3

Brussels' oldest surviving church now curiously incorporates the decapitated tower of the 1134 original as the central section of a bigger Gothic edifice. Behind the palm-tree pulpit, look on the wall above a carved confessional to find a small memorial to 'Petro Brevgello'; ie the artist Pieter Bruegel the Elder, who once lived in nearby Marolles (p122). (Place de la Chapelle; admission free; ⊙9am-7pm Jun-Sep, to 6pm Oct-May; 🚌Anneessens)

Jewish Museum   MUSEUM

4 ⊙ MAP P112, D4

The Jewish Museum hosts good temporary photography exhibits and a permanent collection relating to Jewish life in Belgium and beyond, with a section on the Holocaust. The museum was hit by a terrorist attack in 2014, killing four people; there is stringent security on arrival and the building is protected by armed guards. (☎02-512 19 63; www.aejm.org/members/jewish-museum-of-belgium; Rue des Minimes 21; €8; ⊙10am-5pm Tue-Sat; Ⓜ Louise)

Bibliothèque Royale   LIBRARY

5 ⊙ MAP P112, E2

The city's striking modern library is a beautifully designed space, containing a small museum about books and printing, and a top-floor

Brussels Greeters

A great way of exploring a specific area or indulging in a passion for anything from *gueuze* (lambic) beers to Belgian politics, is to contact Brussels Greeters (www.greeters.be) two weeks before your trip. You fill in a simple online form and the coordinator sets you up with a local who will take you to relevant sights in the city, usually with stops for coffee and lunch along the way (trips take two to four hours). There is no charge for the service, and tips are not accepted.

cafeteria. (www.kbr.be/en; Blvd de l'Empereur 4; ⊙9am-7pm Mon-Fri, to 5pm Sat)

Place du Petit Sablon   PARK

6 ⊙ MAP P112, E4

About 200m uphill from Place du Grand Sablon, this charming little garden is ringed by 48 bronze statuettes representing the medieval guilds. Standing huddled on a fountain plinth like two actors from a Shakespearean drama are Counts Egmont and Hoorn, popular city leaders who were beheaded in the Grand Place in 1568 for defying Spanish rule. The site of Egmont's grand former residence lies behind. (Ⓜ Porte de Namur)

Multitalented Recyclart

A glimpse into 'alternative' Brussels, **Recyclart** (📞02-502 57 34; www.recyclart.be; Rue de Manchester 13-15; 🚉Anneessens) is a graffitied 'arts laboratory' in the old Chapelle station along Rue des Ursulines that revitalised what was once an industrial wasteland. It now hosts cutting-edge gigs, parties with DJs, art installations and theatre productions, and has a daytime cafe; above is a skate park. Its mini-magazine, available in bars across Brussels, lists current events.

Palais Royal
PALACE

9 ⊙ MAP P112, G3

These days Belgium's royal family lives at Laeken, but this sturdy 19th-century palace remains its 'official' residence. One unique room has had its ceiling iridescently clad with the wing cases of 1.4 million Thai jewel beetles by conceptual artist Jan Fabre. You'll also see contemporary royal portraits. It's only open to visitors in summer. (📞02-551 20 20; www.monarchy.be; Place des Palais; admission free; ⏰10.30am-4.30pm Tue-Sun late Jul-early Sep; 🚇Parc)

Musée BELvue
MUSEUM

8 ⊙ MAP P112, F3

Take a chronological audio tour through the airy stuccoed interior of this former royal residence to explore Belgium's history from independence to today, brought to life by exhibits and film footage. Among the artefacts is the jacket worn by Albert I when he died in a climbing accident in 1934. In summer, the restaurant has tables in the pretty garden. (📞070 500 45 54; www.belvue.be; Place des Palais 7; adult/concession €7/6; ⏰for groups with reservation 9.30am-5pm Mon, to 5pm Tue-Fri, 10am-6pm Sat & Sun; 🚇Parc)

Jardin d'Enfants
NOTABLE BUILDING

9 ⊙ MAP P112, B4

Victor Horta's first civic commission, the charming Jardin d'Enfants in the Marolles still functions as a schoolhouse. (Rue St-Ghislain 40; 🚇Porte de Hal)

Coudenberg
ARCHAEOLOGICAL SITE

10 ⊙ MAP P112, F3

Coudenberg Hill (now Place Royale) was the site of Brussels' original 12th-century castle. Over several centuries this was transformed into one of Europe's most elegant and powerful palaces, most notably as the 16th-century residence of Holy Roman Emperor Charles V. Around the palace, courtiers and nobles in turn built fine mansions. The vast complex was destroyed in a catastrophic 1731 fire, but beneath street level the basic structure of the palace's long-hidden lower storeys remains. (www.coudenberg.com; adult/under 26yr/BrusselsCard €7/6/free;

9.30am-5pm Tue-Fri, 10am-6pm Sat & Sun; **M**Parc) .

Palais de Justice
HISTORIC BUILDING

11 ◎ MAP P112, C5

Larger than St Peter's in Rome, this 2.6-hectare complex of law courts was the world's biggest building when it was constructed (1866–83). While the labyrinthine complex is undoubtedly forbidding, it is not easy to secure. Indeed, in several high-profile cases criminals have absconded from its precincts. Behind the building a terrace offers wide panoramas over Brussels' rooftops, with the Atomium and Koekelberg Basilica the stars of the skyline show. A glass **elevator** (Map p112, C5; Rue de l'Epée; admission free; 7.30am-11.45pm; **M**Louise) leads down to the earthy Marolles district. (Place Poelaert; **M**Louise, 92, 94)

Eating

L'Idiot du Village
BELGIAN €€€

12 ✗ MAP P112, C4

Booking ahead is essential to secure a table at this colourful, cosy restaurant, secluded on a little side street near the Place du Jeu-de-Balle flea market. Dishes are rich and aromatic and portions plentiful, considering the cachet of the place. (0487 11 52 18; www.lidiotduvillage.be; Rue Notre Seigneur 19; mains around €30; noon-2pm & 7.30-11pm Wed-Fri, 7.30-10.30pm Tue & Sat; **M**Louise)

Laurent Gerbaud
CAFE €

13 ✗ MAP P112, F2

A bright and welcoming cafe with big picture windows that's perfect for lunch, coffee or hot chocolate if you're between museums. Don't leave without trying the wonderful chocolates, which count as healthy eating in the world of Belgian chocs because they have no alcohol, additives or added sugar. Friendly owner Laurent also runs chocolate-tasting and -making sessions. (02-511 16 02; www.chocolatsgerbaud.be; Rue Ravenstein 2; snacks from €5; 7.30am-7.30pm; **M**Parc)

Claire Fontaine
DELI €

14 ✗ MAP P112, D4

Just off Place du Grand Sablon, this is a tiny but atmospheric tile-floored *épicerie* (deli), fragrant with spices and home-cooked dishes – there's a small kitchen at the back. It's perfect for a nutritious and filling takeaway sandwich or quiche, or you can stock up on oils, wine and boxes of *pain d'épices* (spiced biscuits). (02-512 24 10; Rue Ernest Allard 3; snacks from €6; 11am-7pm Tue-Sat; **M**Porte de Namur)

La Fabrique
CAFE €€

15 ✗ MAP P112, E5

This superbly restored orangery in Parc d'Egmont has huge windows that allow the sunlight to glaze the tables. During the week, it sells healthy lunches like artichoke salad with cheese croquettes and a devilish *suikertaart* (sugar tart).

Brussels Royal Quarter

Mussels in Brussels

Steaming cast-iron pots of mussels (*mosselen* in Dutch, *moules* in French) appear on restaurant tables everywhere. They're traditionally cooked in white wine, with variations such as *à la Provençal* (with tomato) and *à la bière* (in beer and cream), and are accompanied by fries. Mussels were previously only eaten during months with an 'r' in their name, to be assured of their freshness, but modern cultivation techniques now mean mussels from July onwards are considered OK. Never eat any that haven't opened properly once they've been cooked.

Its gargantuan weekend brunch buffet includes roast pumpkin, ricotta and spinach ravioli, smoked salmon with dill and all manner of eggs. (📞02-513 99 48; www.lafabriqueresto.be; Blvd de Waterloo 44; mains €20-30; 🕐11am-4pm Tue-Fri, 10.30am-3.30pm Sat & Sun; Ⓜ️Louise)

Le Perroquet   CAFE €

16 MAP P112, D4

Perfect for a drink, but also good for a simple bite (think salads and variations on croque-monsieurs), this art nouveau cafe with its stained glass, marble tables and timber panelling is an atmospheric, inexpensive stop in an area that's light on such places. Popular with expats. (📞02-512 99 22; Rue Watteeu 31; light meals €9-15; 🕐noon-11.30pm; Ⓜ️Porte de Namur)

Les Brigittines   FRENCH, BELGIAN €€

17 MAP P112, C3

Offering grown-up eating in a muted belle époque dining room, Les Brigittines dishes up traditional French and Belgian food. Its classic (and very meaty) dishes include veal cheek, pigs' trotters and steak tartare. Staff are knowledgeable about local beer and artisanal wines, and can advise on pairing these with your food. (📞02-512 68 91; www.lesbrigittines.com; Place de la Chapelle 5; mains €16-24; 🕐noon-2.30pm & 7-10.30pm Mon-Fri, to 11pm Sat; 📶; Ⓜ️Louise)

Restobières   BELGIAN €€

18 MAP P112, B5

Beer-based twists on typical Belgian meals are served in a delightful if slightly cramped restaurant. The walls are plastered with bottles, grinders and countless antique souvenir biscuit tins featuring Belgian royalty. Try the *carbonade* (beer-based hotpot) or *lapin aux pruneaux* (rabbit with prunes). (📞02-502 72 51; www.restobieres.eu; Rue des Renards 9; mains €12-24, menus €15-38; 🕐noon-3pm & 7-11pm Tue-Sun; Ⓜ️Louise)

Het Warmwater   CAFE €

19 MAP P112, B5

Endearing and friendly little daytime cafe with stencilled teapots and art collages on the walls. The food – croque-monsieurs, salads, cheese and meat platters, and quiches – is simple but satisfying. (www.hetwarmwater.be; Rue des Renards 25; snacks from €5; ☉10am-6pm Thu-Sun; ; ⓂLouise)

Drinking

Brasserie Ploegmans

PUB

20 ⓔ MAP P112, C5

A classic local hostelry with old-fashioned mirror-panelled seats and 1927 chequerboard flooring. It is well regarded for its typical Bruxellois meals (mains €13.50 to 18.50). (https://ploegmans.wordpress.com; Rue Haute 148; mains €13.50-18.50; ☉noon-2.30pm Tue-Fri & 6-10pm Tue-Sat, closed Aug; ⓂLouise)

Fuse

CLUB

21 ⓔ MAP P112, A6

The Marolles club that 'invented' European techno still crams up to 2000 people onto its two dance floors. Once a month it also hosts epic gay night La Démence, a hugely popular rave that attracts men from all over Europe and beyond. (www.fuse.be; Rue Blaes 208; cover €5-12; ☉11pm-7am Sat; ⓂPorte de Hal)

Le Marseillais du Jeu de Balle

BAR

22 ⓔ MAP P112, B5

This traditional corner bar is a much-loved old stager on the square. It serves baguettes and beers, but the speciality is pastis: an anise-flavoured spirit.

Mussels and *frites*

TAMAS SZENDREI/SHUTTERSTOCK ©

What's in a Name?

The Brussels Capital Region comprises the only area in Belgium that's officially bilingual. Bilingualism means that communes, streets, train stations and so on frequently (but not always) have two names, such as the commune of Elsene (in Dutch), which is also known as Ixelles (in French). Street signs list the French, followed by the Dutch, such as 'Petite Rue de la Violette – Korte Violetstraat' (Little Violet St). In French, *rue* (street) comes at the start, in Dutch *straat* is tacked on the end. Marolles signs contain three languages: French, Dutch and the Bruxellois dialect, resulting in mouthfuls such as Rue Haute – Hoogstraat – Op d'Huugstroet (High St). For simplicity, we've used the French names for Brussels.

(📞02-503 00 83; www.facebook.com/lemarseillaisdujeudeballe; Rue Blaes 163; ⏰10am-11pm; Ⓜ Porte de Hal, 🚊Lemonnier)

Entertainment

BOZAR
LIVE MUSIC

23 ⭐ MAP P112, F2

This celebrated classical-music space is home to the National Orchestra and Philharmonic Society. From the outside, the Horta-designed 1928 art deco building is bold rather than enticing, but Henri Le Bœuf Hall is considered to be one of the five best venues in the world for acoustic quality. BOZAR also hosts major art and science exhibitions. (www.bozar.be; Palais des Beaux-Arts, Rue Ravenstein 23; Ⓜ Gare Centrale)

Cinematek
CINEMA

24 ⭐ MAP P112, F2

In a wing of the BOZAR cultural centre, the modern and stylish Cinematek includes a little museum where you can browse archives and memorabilia. The real highlight, though, is the program of silent films screened nearly every day at the cinema, with live piano accompaniment. There's also an impressive program of art-house movies. (📞02-507 83 70; www.cinematheque.be; Rue Baron Horta 9; Ⓜ Gare Centrale)

Théâtre Les Tanneurs
THEATRE

25 ⭐ MAP P112, A4

Sitting on the edge of the Marolles, the theatre is known for dynamic drama and dance. (📞02-512 17 84; www.lestanneurs.be; Rue des Tanneurs 75; Ⓜ Louise)

Shopping

Place du Jeu-de-Balle Flea Market

MARKET

26 MAP P112, B5

The quintessential Marolles experience is haggling at this chaotic flea market, established in 1919. Weekends see it at its liveliest, but for the best bargains, head here early morning midweek. (www.marcheauxpuces.be; Place du Jeu-de-Balle; 6am-2pm Mon-Fri, to 3pm Sat & Sun; M Porte de Hal, Lemonnier)

Pierre Marcolini

CHOCOLATE

27 MAP P112, D3

Rare chocolate beans, experimental flavours (eg tea) and designer black-box packaging make Marcolini's pralines Belgium's hippest and most expensive. (02-512 43 14; www.marcolini.be; Rue des Minimes 1; chocolate per kg €70; 10am-7pm Sun-Thu, to 6pm Fri & Sat; M Porte de Namur)

Sablon Antiques Market

MARKET

28 MAP P112, E4

Over 100 vendors fill this stately square on weekends, selling crockery, crystal, jewellery, furniture, 18th-century Breton Faïence (pottery) and other relics of bygone eras. Prices generally reflect the high quality of the goods for sale. (www.sablon-antiques-market.com; Place du Grand Sablon; 9am-6pm Sat, to 2pm Sun; M Porte de Namur)

Belge une fois

ARTS & CRAFTS

29 MAP P112, C4

Belge une fois is a concept store selling creations by the eponymous designers' collective. It also sells artefacts, accessories and light fixtures by other Belgian designers. Expect everything from simple postcards and concrete cactus holders to large photography prints. (02-503 85 41; www.belgeunefois.com; Rue Haute 89; 11am-6pm Wed-Sat, 1-6pm Sun; 92, 93)

Walking Tour 🥾

A Stroll in the Marolles

Brussels' partially gentrified working-class area, the Marolles, is known for its colourful dialect and down-to-earth watering holes. To appreciate the area's roots, head to Place du Jeu-de-Balle or pop into a neighbourhood bar. Crumbling brick chimneys are another remnant of the area's industrial past. Visit on Sunday for the Gare du Midi market, and to take in morning Mass at the church.

Walking Facts

Start Gare du Midi Market
End L'Idiot du Village
Length 2.1km

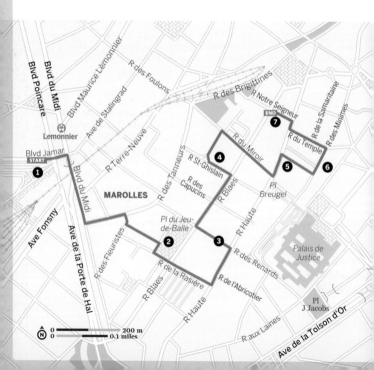

❶ Gare du Midi Market

If you're visiting on a Sunday, head to the **Gare du Midi Market** (Marché du Midi; Gare du Midi; ⏰7am-1pm Sun; Ⓜ Gare du Midi), said to be the biggest in Europe. This sprawl of colourful stalls next to the railway lines has an international flavour, with exotic North African and Mediterranean spices, cheeses, meats, clothing and leather goods.

❷ Jeu-de-Balle Flea Market

Haggle at this popular, chaotic flea market (p121). The best bargains are to be had early on weekday mornings. Stop for a coffee at Le Marseillais (p119) on the northeast corner of the square: 55 varieties of pastis are served here.

❸ Rue des Renards

Narrow Rue des Renards exemplifies how the area is changing – on the right, heading downhill, are galleries and antique stores; on the left cottages and traditional restaurants. You'll may find a vestige of the old Marolles here: a cart selling little pots of snails.

❹ Jardin d'Enfants

This lovely Horta building (p116) is a school, so you'll only be able to view it from the outside. Look for sinuous plant motifs, a playful tower and stripes of grey and pale stone.

❺ Brueghel House

There is a museum in this step-gabled **house** (☎02-513 89 40; Rue Haute 132; Ⓜ Louise) where Pieter Bruegel the Elder lived and died, but it's only open by reservation; phone ahead or check with the tourist office for details.

❻ St-Jean-et-Étienne aux Minimes

The area's **church** (Rue des Minimes 62) is a huge, sooty and weather-beaten baroque structure, completed in 1715. If you visit on Sunday at 11.30am, you can go to Mass – the acoustics of the ribbed cupola are very good, and Mass features either Gregorian chants or Bach cantatas.

❼ L'Idiot du Village

Booking ahead to secure a table at the colourful L'Idiot du Village (p117), secluded on a little sidestreet north of the Place du Jeu-de-Balle. The Belgian dishes are rich and aromatic (lots of herbs) and portions are generous. If you're here on a day when the restaurant is closed, drop in to friendly neighbourhood café Het Warmwater (p118) instead.

Explore ◈
EU Quarter & Etterbeek

There are plenty of sights in the EU Quarter to entice visitors, notably the museums grouped around leafy Parc du Cinquantenaire (p126) and the fine early-20th-century houses that fringe Square Marie-Louise (p132). It also has a reputation for office blocks and thundering traffic and is, of course, the heart of European politics, although whether that's an enticement or a deterrent will depend on your point of view.

Drop into the EU Parliament (p131) for its 10am tour or take a stroll around Parc Léopold (p132), before walking with the dinosaurs at the spectacular Musée des Sciences Naturelles (p131). Head to the Parc du Cinquantenaire for lofty views accessed via the military museum. Nearby you can see the glinting facade of the art nouveau Maison Cauchie (p127) before wandering over to Square Marie-Louise, surrounded by elegant apartment blocks. Come the evening, Place Jourdan offers some good eating spots, including a legendary frites (chips) stand.

Getting There & Around

Ⓜ The closest stop for the museums is Mérode, while to explore the EU sights head to Schuman. For Square Marie-Louise get off at Maelbeek.

🏃 The EU Parliament is a pleasant half-hour walk form Grand Place; you can cross the Parc du Bruxelles en route.

Neighbourhood Map on p130

The blue-glass EU Parliament (p131) TRABANTOS/SHUTTERSTOCK ©

Top Sight 📷
Parc du Cinquantenaire

Parc du Cinquantenaire was built during Léopold II's reign. It's best known for its cluster of museums – art, history, military and motor vehicles – which house an incredible 350,000 artefacts. The Musée Art & Histoire (p128) in the southern wing of the Cinquantenaire buildings is chock-a-block with antiquities. Autoworld, in the northern building, has a huge collection of vintage cars.

◎ MAP P130, E3

Rue de la Loi & Rue Belliard

Ⓜ Mérode

Cinquantenaire

The **Cinquantenaire** itself (pictured) is a vast triumphal arch reminiscent of Paris' Arc de Triomphe. It was designed to celebrate Belgium's 50th anniversary (*cinquantenaire* in French) in 1880, but it took so long to build that by that date only a temporary plaster version was standing. The arch was completed in 1905.

Autoworld

Prior to WWII, Belgium had a thriving auto industry, and the coolest of car collections on display at **Autoworld** (www.autoworld.be; adult/concession/ BrusselsCard €10/€7/free; ⏱10am-6pm Apr-Sep, to 5pm Oct-Mar) is its legacy. Here you can see 400 vehicles (Model T Fords, Citroën 2CVs and more, through to the 1970s), housed in a stunning 1880 steel structure. Notice the Harley Davidson the present king gifted to Belgium's police force when his biker days were over.

Musée Royal de l'Armée et d'Histoire Militaire

One for military buffs, the **Royal Museum of the Armed Forces & Military History** (☏02-737 78 11; www.klm-mra.be; admission free; ⏱10am-6pm Tue-Sun) houses an extensive array of weaponry, uniforms, vehicles, warships, paintings and documentation dating from the Middle Ages to Belgian independence and the mid-20th century.

Maison Cauchie

This stunning 1905 **house** (Map p130, E4; ☏02-733 86 84; www.cauchie.be; Rue des Francs 5; adult/ child €7/free; ⏱10am-1pm & 2-5.30pm 1st Sat & Sun of month) was the home of architect and painter Paul Cauchie (1875–1952). Its facade, adorned with graceful female figures, is one of the most beautiful in Brussels. It looks like a Klimt painting transformed into architecture. A petition saved the house from demolition in 1971, and since 1975 it has been a protected monument. If you can't visit, the facade alone warrants a visit.

★ Top Tips

o The top of the Cinquantenaire arch provides sweeping city views. You access it via the military museum either by steps or a lift.

o In the park itself, look out for the **Pavillon Horta-Lambeaux** (Map p130, D2) the northwest. You won't find any of the architect's trademark motifs in this rather solid neoclassical structure, though: it was his first public commission.

✕ Take a Break

There's a great collection of cafes, restaurants and bars on Place Jourdan, including the city's most famous frites stand, Maison Antoine (p133).

Otherwise, try ice cream joint Capoue (p135).

Top Sight 📷
Musée Art & Histoire

This rich collection ranges from ancient Egyptian sarcophagi and Meso-American masks to icons and wooden bicycles. Decide what you want to see before coming or the sheer scope can prove overwhelming. Visually attractive spaces include the medieval stone carvings set around a neo-Gothic cloister and the soaring Corinthian columns (convincing fibreglass props) that bring atmosphere to an original AD 420 mosaic from Roman Syria.

◎ MAP P130, E3

📞 02-741 73 01

www.artandhistory.
museum

Parc du Cinquantenaire 10

adult/child/BrusselsCard
€10/4/free

🕙 9.30am-5pm Tue-Fri,
from 10am Sat & Sun

Ⓜ Mérode

Antiquity

The rich variety of antiquities ranges from ancient Egyptian treasures, including 10 mummies and sarcophagi, to a large collection of Belgian artefacts from the first human settlements in the region. The highlight, though, is the Roman Syrian gallery, where a large and vivid AD 415 mosaic depicts tigers being speared and lions being hunted down by dogs.

European Decorative Arts

Many people will make a beeline for the glorious art nouveau and art deco objects, whose display cases were designed by Victor Horta. There are also Romanesque, Renaissance and baroque galleries, and a changing collection of tapestries. A whole gallery is devoted to clocks and astronomical devices, and there's also a delightful assemblage of 35 painted sledges from the 1930s and '40s.

Non-European Civilisations

The scope of this section is impressive, taking in pre-Columbian art; Native American headdresses; Jainist, Hindu and Buddhist deities; Chinese ceramics; rare Islamic textiles; Byzantine art; and Coptic fabrics. Perhaps the most startling exhibit, though, is the woefully displaced Easter Island sculpture, a 6-tonne stone giant collected on a Franco-Belgian expedition in the 1930s.

Tintin

The museum is a must for those on the Tintin trail: a ghoulish skeleton mummy inspired *The Seven Crystal Balls,* while the Arumba fetish in *The Broken Ear* was based on a wooden votive figure displayed in the galleries.

★ Top Tips

○ Labelling in this museum is in French and Dutch, so the English-language audioguide (€3 extra) is worth considering.

○ Free admission after 1pm on the first Wednesday of the month.

○ The museum shop sells scholarly guides to the gallery collections, as well as the usual memorabilia and gifts.

✕ Take a Break

The museum has an upmarket bistro, **Le Midi Cinquante** (☑ 02-735 87 54; www.kmkg-mrah.be/restaurant-le-midi-50; mains €13-15; ⏱ 9.30am-4.30pm, closed Mon), whose terrace looks onto the park.

L'Atelier Européen (Map p130, C2; ☑ 02-734 91 40; www.atelier-euro.be; Rue Franklin 28; mains €14-29; ⏱ noon-2.30pm & 7-10.30pm Mon-Fri; Ⓜ Schuman) is a pleasant French-Belgian place close by.

Brussels EU Quarter & Etterbeek

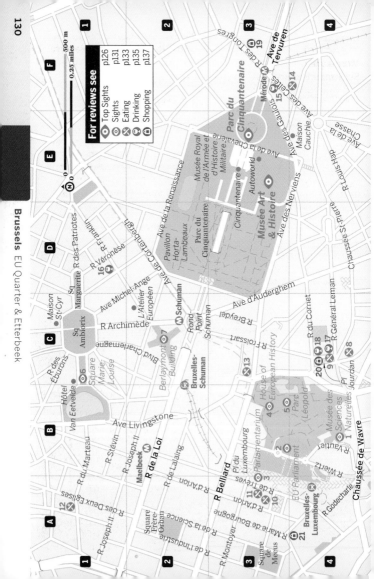

For reviews see

◎	Top Sights	p126
◉	Sights	p131
✖	Eating	p133
◆	Drinking	p135
◉	Shopping	p137

500 m
0.25 miles

Sights

Musée des Sciences Naturelles

MUSEUM

1 ◉ MAP P130, B4

Thought-provoking and highly interactive, this museum has far more than the usual selection of stuffed animals. But the undoubted highlight is a unique 'family' of iguanodons – 10m-high dinosaurs found in a Hainaut coal mine in 1878. A computer simulation shows the mudslide that might have covered them, sand-boxes allow you to play dino hunter and multilingual videos give a wonderfully nuanced debate on recent palaeontology. (☎02-627 42 11; www.naturalsciences.be; Rue Vautier 29; adult/concession/child/Brussels-Card €7/6/4.50/free; ⏰9.30am-5pm Tue-Fri, 10am-6pm Sat & Sun; 🚌38)

EU Parliament

NOTABLE BUILDING

2 ◉ MAP P130, B3

Inside this decidedly dated blue-glass building (completed only just over a decade ago) political junkies can sit in on a parliamentary session in the huge debating chamber known as the hemicycle, or tour it when parliament's not sitting. Tours of the complex are via multilingual headphones. (☎02-284 34 57; www.europarl.europa.eu; Rue Wiertz 43; admission free; ⏰tours 10am & 3pm Mon-Thu, 10am Fri; 🚌38, ⓂTrône)

Musée des Sciences Naturelles

Parlamentarium VISITOR CENTRE

3 ⊙ MAP P130, A3

The visitor centre of the EU Parliament makes a valiant multimedia attempt to engage visitors, with an interactive floor map allowing you to tour the EU, profiles of members of the parliament and a discussion room. There's a one-hour scavenger hunt for kids. (www.europarl.europa.eu/visiting/en/brussels/parlamentarium; Place du Luxembourg 100; admission free; ◷1-6pm Mon, 9-6pm Tue-Fri, 10am-6pm Sat & Sun; ☐38, Ⓜ Trône)

House of European History MUSEUM

4 ⊙ MAP P130, B3

Housed in the beautifully renovated Eastman Building, this elegant new museum takes you into some dark corners of European history, from war and destruction to the biggest peace project ever endeavoured. There are detours from this tumultuous path for Dutch tulips, English football and European cuisine, the latter only described in broadbrush terms. The highly (perhaps overly) interactive experience takes about 1½ hours, with permanent and temporary exhibitions that you can roam through in 24 languages. (HoEH; http://historia-europa.ep.eu; Rue Belliard 135; admission free; ◷1-6pm Mon, 9am-6pm Tue-Fri, 10am-6pm Sat & Sun; ☐21, 27, 59, 60, 80)

Parc Léopold PARK

5 ⊙ MAP P130, B3

Steep-sloping Parc Léopold was Brussels Zoo until 1880 and now forms an unexpectedly pleasant oasis, hidden away just behind the EU Parliament. (Ⓜ Schuman)

Square Marie-Louise SQUARE

6 ⊙ MAP P130, C1

You can feed the ducks in the pretty tree-lined pond surrounded by greenery and a smattering of

Art Nouveau in the EU Quarter

Private **Hôtel van Eetvelde** (Map p130, C1; Ave Palmerston 2-4; Ⓜ Schuman) can only be accessed on an ARAU (p22) tour. While the outside of this building is not Brussels' most gripping, its interior is a Horta masterpiece studded with exotic timbers and sporting a central glass dome infused with African inspired plant motifs. Its owner, Baron Van Eetvelde, was at that time Minister for the Congo and, not coincidentally, the country's highest-paid civil servant. Narrow **Maison St-Cyr** (Map p130, C1; Sq Ambiorix 11; Ⓜ Schuman) has a classic 1903 facade that's remarkable for its naturalistic copper-framed window, filigree balconies and a circular upper portal. It's crowned by a devil-may-care topknot of extravagantly twisted ironwork.

art nouveau architecture. (off Ave Palmerston; M Maelbeek)

Berlaymont Building

NOTABLE BUILDING

7 ⊙ MAP P130, C2

The European Commission, the EU's sprawling bureaucracy, centres on the vast, four-winged Berlaymont building. Built in 1967, it's striking but by no means beautiful, despite a billion-euro rebuild between 1991 and 2004 that removed asbestos-tainted construction materials. Information panels dotted around the building give insight into the history of this neighbourhood and Brussels' international role. The building is not open to the public. (Rue de la Loi 200; M Schuman)

Eating

Stirwen

FRENCH €€€

8 ⊗ MAP P130, C4

This long-established Franco-Belgian restaurant is popular with a discerning EU crowd. The decor is rather dark and conservative, but the classic and traditional French cooking is always reliable. (☑02-640 85 41; www.stirwen.be; Chaussée St-Pierre 15; mains €28-36; ⊗noon-midnight Mon-Fri; M Schuman)

Maison Antoine

BELGIAN €

9 ⊗ MAP P130, C4

Brussels can be divided into two kinds of people: not French- and Dutch-speaking, or locals and ex-

pats, but rather those who swear by this chip shop, and those who pledge allegiance to the caravan on Place Flagey in Ixelles. Antoine's chips are twice-fried in beef fat, and you'll see dignitaries and the odd celeb queuing for a coneful. (☑02-230 54 56; www.maisonantoine. be; Place Jourdan; chips €2.60-3; ⊗11.30am-1am Sun-Thu, to 2am Fri & Sat; M Schuman)

Cafe Luxembourg

CAFE €

10 ⊗ MAP P130, A3

Featuring a leather and copper interior, this *café* offers a range of quinoa-based superbowls and other market-fresh nibbles for lunch. Its terrace gets seriously packed on Thursdays when loose-tied Eurocrats sip after-work Wasatinis (vodka with wasabi) and craft beers. On weekends, the wallet-friendly brunch boasts a killer banana-raspberry French toast, velvety scrambled eggs and freshly pressed juices. (☑02-721 57 15; www.cafeluxembourg.be; Place du Luxembourg 10; lunch €10-15, brunch €14-17; ⊗8am-1am Mon & Tue, to 3am Wed-Fri, 10am-3am Sat, 11am-midnight Sun; ☒12, 21, 22, 27, 34, 38, 64, 80, 95)

Domenica

ITALIAN €

11 ⊗ MAP P130, A3

Selling honest, ethically sourced lunches to a predominantly Eurocrat crowd, Domenica holds up its values of quality and sustainability with homemade lasagne, stunning truffle pizzas made from

French Fries – Or Are They? 🍽

Just as the Brussels waffle actually originates from Ghent, French fries (frites) in fact hail from Belgium. The misnomer evolved during WWI in West Flanders, when English officers heard their Belgian counterparts speaking French while consuming fries and mistook their nationality (military orders were given in French, even to Dutch-only-speaking soldiers, with tragic consequences).

Fries here are made from Belgian- or Netherlands-grown bintje potatoes. They're hand-cut about 1cm thick – any smaller and they absorb too much oil and burn – and cooked first at a lower temperature, then again at a higher temperature to become crispy on the outside while remaining soft inside. This double-cooking is what distinguished the Belgian chip from its flabbier counterparts elsewhere.

Typically, frites are served in a paper cone and liberally smothered in a rich sauce. There are dozens of sauces, including the classic, mayonnaise. If you're bewildered by the choice, take a chance with Andalouse, which is like very mildly spiced thousand-island dressing.

24-hour slow-rise doughs, and a small selection of vegan chocolates. Gourmets should fill their grocery baskets with creamy balls of Pugliese burrata and bottles of organic wine. (📞02-657 30 67; www.domenica.eu.com; Rue de Trèves 32b; mains €3.50-€8.50; ⏰8am-7pm Mon-Fri; 🚌12, 21, 22, 27, Ⓜ Trône)

Les 4 jeudis   VEGETARIAN €€

12 ❌ MAP P130, A1

Veritable vegetarian delights are served up at Les 4 jeudis, a sun-baked corner restaurant where the chef's elaborate lacto-fermented processes are said to keep the nutrients packed into organic dishes like citrus-marinated vegie carpaccio served with cajou and goji berries sauce, or the

creamy apple and date mousse topped with chocolate crumble. (📞02-721 10 49; https://les4jeudis.be/en; Rue du Marteau 36a; mains €10-25; ⏰noon-4pm Tue-Fri; 🛜📶; Ⓜ Madou)

Grand Central   BUFFET €

13 ❌ MAP P130, C3

Spread out across two floors, this huge bar-restaurant packs in the crowds with its buffet lunches and dinners. Expect slow-roasted aubergines, tomatoes with white beans and all manner of healthy salads to accompany ribs and steaks that have been cooked on a wood-fired grill, along with fresh fish. The on-site barista is something of a coffee Picasso too. (www.legrandcentral.com; Rue Belliard 190;

mains €12; ⊙9am-midnight Mon-Fri, 10am-midnight Sat, to 7.30pm Sun; MSchuman)

Capoue
ICE CREAM €

14 ⊗ MAP P130, F4

Great ice cream in a dizzying variety of flavours, including *speculoos*, Belgium's trademark biscuit. It also serves frozen yoghurt and snacks. (☎02-705 37 10; www.capoue.com; Ave des Celtes 36; ⊙1-10pm; MMérode)

Drinking

La Terrasse
PUB

15 ⊕ MAP P130, F3

Handy for the Cinquantenaire, this wood-panelled classic *café* has a tree-shaded terrace and

makes an ideal refreshment stop after a hard day's museuming. Snacks, pancakes, ice creams, breakfasts (from €3.90) and decent pub meals (€10 to €18) are all available at various times. Try the 'beer of the month'. (☎02-732 28 51; www.brasserielaterrasse.be; Ave des Celtes 1; beers €2.40-4.50; ⊙8am-midnight Mon-Sat, from 10am Sun; MMérode)

Piola Libri
BAR

16 ⊕ MAP P130, D1

Italian Eurocrats relax after work on sofas, at pavement tables or in the tiny triangle of back garden and enjoy free tapas-style snacks with chilled white wines at this convivial bookshop-*café*-bar. It has an eclectic program of readings and DJ nights. (☎02-736 93 91;

Grand Central

Are You
Breaking up with Me?

It's perhaps an irony that Belgium, with its central role in the – ideally – consensual politics of the European Commission and NATO, is linguistically and culturally at odds with itself. Nowhere is this split more evident than in bilingual Brussels, where there is real division between the numerically dominant French speakers and the proud Flemish residents.

In 2006, francophone public broadcaster RTBF interrupted programming with footage of a reporter outside the Royal Palace, claiming that Flanders had declared independence and King Albert had left the country. Only after half an hour did the program-makers admit the hoax, stating that they intended to demonstrate the importance of ongoing political debate for the future of Belgium.

The question if Belgium will hold together or split apart is never far away. Brussels – with its geographical location in Flanders, its primary linguistic orientation in Wallonia, and its status as the capital of the EU – is the major sticking point. There is also the question of what would happen to Belgium's tiny German-speaking region, as well as the fate of Belgium's monarchy, although surveys have shown that many younger Belgians believe a monarchy is unnecessary in the 21st century.

If Belgium did split, it's unlikely that Wallonia would join France, or that Flanders would join the Netherlands (though Dutch citizens overwhelmingly support Flanders becoming part of their country). Instead, one model for the future is that Flanders and Wallonia would each become independent, with Brussels becoming its own city-state, possibly administered by the EU. Certainly, the economic and legal unification provided by the EU makes it more viable than at any other time in modern history for such small nations to exist independently.

Still, the general sentiment in most quarters is that people don't want Belgium to split. Aside from personal attachment, a key pragmatic reason is that 'Belgian' has become a trademark, with considerable international standing as a byword for quality (such as 'Belgian chocolate' or 'Belgian beer'). Some feel this reputation may be diminished if Flanders and Wallonia split into separate countries, since these are lesser-known names internationally. For the foreseeable future at least, it seems likely that Belgium will endure.

www.piolalibri.be; Rue Franklin 66; ⏰noon-8pm Mon-Fri, to 6pm Sat, closed Aug; 📶; Ⓜ Schuman)

L'Autobus
BAR

17 🚇 MAP P130, C4

This old-timers' bar is opposite Maison Antoine (p133), the city's most famous *friture* (*frites* shop). The owners don't mind if you demolish a cone of *frites* while downing a beer or two. On Sunday it's a breather for vendors from the Place Jourdan food market. (📞02-230 63 16; Place Jourdan; Ⓜ Schuman)

OR Coffee
COFFEE

18 🚇 MAP P130, C4

Coffee geeks rejoice: this speciality espresso bar, which roasts its own beans, serves some of the best caffeine in the city. Among battered sofas, blackboards and unwieldy greenery, the owners host cuppings (coffee tastings) and workshops and can advise on the origins of its Arabica coffee. (📞09-336 37 36; www.orcoffee. be; Place Jourdan 13; ⏰8am-5pm Mon-Fri, from 9am Sat & Sun; 📶; Ⓜ Schuman)

Shopping

Neuhaus
CHOCOLATE

19 🔒 MAP P130, F3

This chocolatier originated in the Galeries Royales, and everything is still made near Brussels; it invented the praline back in 1912. It sells chocolate, biscuits and delicious ice cream. (📞02-734 46 64; Rue des Tongres 43; ⏰10am-6.30pm; Ⓜ Mérode)

Place Jourdan Market
MARKET

20 🔒 MAP P130, C4

Place Jourdan hosts a small Sunday-morning market selling food and clothes. (Place Jourdan; ⏰7am-2pm Sun; Ⓜ Schuman)

Crush Wine
WINE

21 🔒 MAP P130, A4

A wondrous cellar stocking over 190 Australian wines (the most comprehensive selection in Europe). Look out for rare drops from Tasmania and deliberate over dozens of Margaret River reds. There are daily tastings and tapas and regular wine events; call ahead for the schedule of Saturday openings. (📞02-502 66 97; www.crushwine.be; Rue Caroly 39; ⏰11am-7pm Mon-Fri, plus 1 Sat per month; Ⓜ Trône)

Top Sights 📷
Musée Horta

The typically austere exterior doesn't give much away, but Victor Horta's former home (designed and built between 1898 and 1901) is an art nouveau jewel. The museum is located in the neigbourhood of Saint-Gilles, south of most other Brussels sights.

◉ MAP P76

📞 02-543 04 90

www.hortamuseum.be

Rue Américaine 25

adult/child €10/3

🕑 2-5.30pm Tue-Sun

Ⓜ Horta, 🚊 91, 92

Stairwell

The stairwell is the structural triumph of the house – follow the playful knots and curlicues of the banister, which become more exuberant as you ascend, ending at a tangle of swirls and glass lamps at the skylight, glazed with plain and citrus-coloured glass.

Dining Room

Floor mosaics, glittering stained glass and ceramic-brick walls reflect the light in the superbly harmonious dining room, rich with swirling American-ash furniture, glowing brass and a pink-and-orange colour scheme.

Bedrooms

Follow the elaborate twists and turns of the banister upstairs to the bedrooms. Horta's daughter's room has a pretty winter garden, while you can only envy people who were invited to stay in the guest bedroom at the top of the house: the swirly brass door handle is a pleasure in itself.

Exterior Details

As is typical of Horta's work, the exterior is relatively austere, though nice to contemplate once you've been inside. Look out for the dragonfly-shaped railing of the guestroom window and the industrial metal balcony.

★ **Top Tips**

o Visits are limited to 45 people at a time; arrive early to avoid queuing.

o For detailed coverage buy the excellent museum guide (€10).

o Guided tours in English are available on request.

o Another option for seeing the house – and other art nouveau buildings – is with an expert guide on an ARAU (p22) tour.

✗ **Take a Break**

Seafood restaurant **La Quincaillerie** (☎ 02-533 98 33; www. quincaillerie.be; Rue du Page 45; mains €19-38; ◷ noon-2.30pm Mon-Sat, 7pm-midnight daily; M Horta) sits close by.

Or have an ice cream at **Le Framboisier** (☎ 02-647 51 44; www. leframboisierdoré.be; Rue du Bailli 35; ◷ 1-7pm; M Louise).

Brussels Top Sight

Survival Guide

Bruxelles-Central (p144) LAURA ZAMBON/SHUTTERSTOCK ©

Before You Go

Book Your Stay

Accommodation availability varies markedly by season and area. May to September occupancy is very high (especially at weekends) along the coast and in Bruges. However, those same weekends you'll find business hotels cutting prices in Brussels. Many but by no means all options include breakfast. National taxes are included in quoted prices. It's worth booking accommodation ahead, especially B&Bs and smaller hotels, which don't always have receptions.

Useful Websites

Les Auberges de Jeunesse (www.lesauber gesdejeunesse.be) Affiliated with Hostelling International.

Vlaamse Jeugd-herbergen (www.youthhostels.be) Also affiliated with Hostelling International.

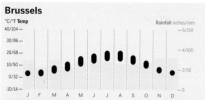

Brussels

°C/°F **Temp**

Rainfall inches/mm

When to Go

○ High Season (Jul–Aug) Sunny, warm weather, means overloaded hotels in Bruges and the Belgian Coast, but bargains can be found in Brussels.

○ Shoulder Season (May, Jun & Sep) Pleasant weather

is reasonably likely; slightly cheaper room rates in Bruges.

○ Low Season (Oct–Mar) Weather often cold and wet with some attractions closed in Bruges, but the best yearly room rates to be found.

Gîtes d'Étape (www.gitesdetape.be) Hostel-style accommodation.

Bed&Breakfasts BeNeLux (http://bedandbreakfast.be) Official B&B listings.

Logeren in Vlaanderen (www.logereninvlaanderen.be) Apartments and holiday homes in rural Flanders.

Camping.be (https://www.camping.be) Campground finder.

Best Budget

Train Hostel (☏02-808 61 76; www.trainhostel.be/en; Ave Georges Rodenbach 6, Brussels; dm/d/ste €18/45/129; ☏; ☐58, 58, ☐7, 92, ☐Schaerbeek) Sleep in a beautifully revamped train carriage.

Villa Botanique Guesthouse (☏0496 59 93 79; http://villabota niqueguesthouse.be; Chaussée de Haecht 31, Brussels; dm €30, d €60; ☏; ☐Botanique) Mansion living on a budget.

Bauhaus (St Christopher's Hostel; ☏050-34 10 93; www.bauhaus.be; Langestraat 133-137, Bruges; dm/d from €21/39; @☏) This backpacker village incorporates a hostel, apartments, a nightclub and internet cafe.

Best Midrange

B&B Dieltiens

(☑ 050-33 42 94; www.bedandbreakfastbruges.be; Waalsestraat 40, Bruges; s/d/tr from €70/80/90; ☏) Art fills this superbly central yet quiet restored classical mansion.

Chambres d'Hôtes du Vaudeville

(☑ 0484 59 46 69; www.theatredu vaudeville.be; Galerie de la Reine 11, Brussels; d from €120; ☏ ; ☐ Bruxelles Central) Follow in Victor Hugo's footstep and stay in a 19th-century gallery.

Living in Brûsel

(☑ 0497 57 24 27; www.livinginbrusel.be; Ave de la Chasse 132, Brussels; d from €135; ☏ ; Ⓜ Thieffry) Great views and friendly people at this stone-built townhouse.

Best Top End

Vintage Hotel

(☑ 02-533 99 80; www.vintage hotel.be; Rue Dejoncker 45, Brussels; d from €65, caravan from €135; ☏ ; Ⓜ Louise) The quirkiest option in town: glamp it up in an Airstream caravan.

Hôtel Le Dixseptième

(☑ 02-517 17 17; www.ledixseptieme.be; Rue de la Madeleine 25, Brussels; d €130-190, ste €200-370; ❄ ☏ ; ☐ Bruxelles Central) Four-poster beds and luxury living at one of the city's grandest hotels.

Hôtel Métropole

(☑ 02-217 23 00, reservations 02-214 24 24; www.metropolehotel.com; Place de Brouckère 31, Brussels; d €170-350, weekend rates from €130; ☺ ❄ ☏ ; Ⓜ De Brouckère) A marbled and glamorous option with live music in the bar.

Arriving in Bruges & Brussels

Air

Brussels Airport

(https://www.brussels airport.be/en) Located 14km northeast of Brussels. There are ATMs on most levels, and for stamps there's a post point in the Louis Delhaize grocery shop. The arrivals hall (Level 2) has currency exchange, car-rental agencies and tourist information. The bus terminus and luggage lockers are on Level 0, the train station on Level 1.

Brussels South Charleroi Airport

(www.brussels-charle roi-airport.com) Brussels' second airport, is 46km southeast of the city and is used mainly by budget airlines, including Ryanair.

Bus

Bruges

Intercity and international bus services originate and terminate at the bus interchange at **Bruges Central Station** (Stationsplein 5).

Eurolines (☑ 02-669 20 07; www.eurolines.eu) Nightly buses to London (from €30). Tickets must be booked by phone or online.

Brussels

Eurolines (☑ 02-274 13 50; www.eurolines.be; Rue du Progrès 80; ☐ Gare du Nord) Operates services to London, Amsterdam, Paris and other international destinations from **Bruxelles-Nord station** (Gare du Nord). **TEC Bus W (for Waterloo)** (🚍W)

Train

Bruxelles-Midi (Gare du Midi; luggage office per article per day €4, luggage lockers per 24hr small/large €3/4; ⏱ luggage office 6am-9pm; Ⓜ Gare du Midi, 🚆 Bruxelles-Midi) is the main station for international connections: the Eurostar, TGV and Thalys high-speed trains (prebooking compulsory) stop here. Most other mainline trains stop in quick succession at Bruxelles-Midi, **Bruxelles-Central** (Gare Centrale; Map p84, G5) and, except for Amsterdam trains, at **Bruxelles-Nord** (Gare du Nord). Information offices at all three stations open early morning to late evening. For all enquiries, consult www.belgiantrain.be/en or call 🕿02-555 25 55.

Bruges' train station is 1.5km south of Markt. Twice-hourly trains run to Kortrijk (€8.10, 40 minutes) and to Brussels (€14.50, one hour) via Ghent (€7, 23 minutes).

Getting Around

Car & Motorcycle Best avoided in both Bruges and Brussels: the slightest hiccup on either ring road brings traffic to a halt, especially on Friday afternoons.

Bicycle Brussels boasts a network of bike lanes and separate bike paths while Bruges is less bike-friendly with heavy foot-traffic and mainly bumpy, cobblestoned streets.

Public Transport Brussels' excellent integrated bus-tram-metro system is operated by **STIB/MIVB** (🕿 02-515 20 00; www.stib.be; ⏱ 10am-6pm Mon-Sat). It runs from about 6am to midnight. Bruges city buses are operated by **DeLijn** (🕿 070 220 200; www.delijn.be/en) and run from 5.30am to 11pm. **NMBS/SNCB** (🕿 02-528 28 28; www.belgianrail. be) operates regular 'B' trains between Brussels and Ostend (€18, 1⅓ hours)

Kusttram DeLijn operates this tram that

runs along the coast between Knokke-Heist and De Panne/Adinkerke, serving every town on the coast. It departs every 15 to 30 minutes between sunrise and midnight. The full route takes just over two hours; it's the longest tram line in the world.

Rollerblades Belgium is perhaps unique in having special road rules for 'rollers' (those on rollerblades or rollerskates).

Taxi Official taxis run meters and have standard fares.

Essential Information

Accessible Travel

Although cobblestones are a literal pain in the backside for wheelchair users, the cities are well endowed with kerb cuts, tactile paving, audible signals at pedestrian crossings, wheelchair-accessible taxis and assistance in the metro and on trains. Most public transport and major tourist attractions are accessible, but many shops in ancient buildings are not. There is a good stock of accessible accommodation, even at the budget end.

Download Lonely Planet's free accessible travel guides from https://shop.lonely planet.com/categories/accessible-travel.

Bruges

Although cobblestones in Bruges can present a challenge, neighbourhoods outside the centre are more wheelchair-friendly.

You will find everything you need to know – about accommodation, sights and activities, transport, care and assistance – from Visit Flanders (www.visitflanders.com/en/accessibility). There are downloadable brochures on a broad range of topics from day trips for vision-impaired visitors to accessible holiday accommodation, as well as an accessible Bruges map.

Brussels

Travellers to Brussels who have access needs are in luck: the country's tourism management bodies are among the most progressive in the world and have produced a wealth of information to help plan your trip and enjoy your stay. The **Accessible Travel Info Point** (☏070 23 30 50; www.accessinfo.be; Rue du Marché aux Herbes 61; ☉9am-6pm Mon-Sat, 10am-5pm Sun; 🚇Bourse) website has a wealth of information on transport, accommodation and things to see and do.

Brussels Airport (https://www.brussels airport.be/en/passn gr/reduced-mobility) is completely accessible, with lifts throughout and accessible eating places.

The following are useful links for those arriving by train:

Eurostar (www.euro star.com/uk-en/travel-info/travel-planning/accessibility)

SNCB (www.belgianrail.be/en/customer-ser vice/passengers-with-reduced-mobility.aspx)

Thalys (https://www.thalys.com/be/en/services/before/your-train-journey#disabled-passengers)

Fifty metro and pre-metro stations have been fully adapted for those with reduced mobility, and several bus lines offer a low floor, kneeling system and an access ramp. STIB's Taxibus (www.stib-mivb.be/taxibus.html?l=en) offers door-to-door transport for disabled persons upon request.

Business Hours

Many sights close on Monday. Restaurants normally close one full day per week. Opening hours for shops, bars and cafes vary widely.

Banks 8.30am–3.30pm or later Monday to Friday, some also Saturday morning

Bars 10am–1am, but hours are very flexible

Restaurants noon–2.30pm and 7pm–9.30pm

Shops 10am–6.30pm Monday to Saturday, sometimes closed for an hour at lunchtime

Discount Cards

Bruges

If you're visiting more than a couple of city museums, consider purchasing a **Musea Brugge Card** (concession/adult €22/28) which gives free entry to all museums operated by the city of Bruges (www.visitbruges.be/16-locations) over a three-day period. Passes cannot be purchased online: just ask for a Musea Brugge card at your first port of call.

Brussels

The cheapest way to see several top sites in Brussels is with the **BrusselsCard** (www.brusselscard.be; 24/48/72hr €26/34/42). The card gets you into 40 major museums and provides free city transport plus discounts for other attractions and some shops and restaurants. It's available through tourist offices, STIB agencies and larger museums.

On the first Wednesday afternoon of each month, most of Brussels' major museums are free to enter.

The Arsène50 (p149) office at the tourist office offers heavily discounted tickets for cultural events.

Electricity

Type C
220V/50Hz

Type E
220V/50Hz

Emergencies

- **Emergency** 📞112
- **Police** 📞101

LGBT+

Attitudes to homosexuality are pretty laid-back in Belgium. Same-sex couples have been able to wed legally since 2003, and since 2006 have had the same rights enjoyed by heterosexual couples, including inheritance and adoption.

Bruges

Bruges' gay scene is notoriously fickle, due to a tight-knit local community, proximity to the larger gay centres of Antwerp and Brussels and the sheer volume of non-resident visitors. There are a handful of friendly bars here but no banging nightlife to speak of.

Try www.gayscout.com or www.travelgay.com for listings.

Brussels

Brussels' compact but thriving Rainbow Quarter centres on Rue du Marché au

Charbon. Here you'll find a dozen gay-oriented *cafés* – try **Stammbar** (☏ 0471 80 14 39; http://stammbar.be; Rue du Marché au Charbon 114; ☺ 9pm-1am Mon-Sat, to 3am Sun; ▣ Annees-sens) – and two LGBT+ information centres/bars: the thriving and multilingual **Rainbow House** (☏ 02-503 59 90; www.rainbowhouse.be; Rue du Marché au Charbon 42; ☺ 6.30-10.30pm Wed-Sat; ▣ Anneessens) and Francophone **Tels Quels** (☏ 02-512 32 34; www.telsquels.be; Rue du Marché au Charbon 81; ☺ from 5pm Sun-Tue, Thu & Fri, from 2pm Wed & Sat; ▣ Anneessens), which runs telephone helpline **Telégal** (☏ 02-502 07 00; ☺ 8pm-midnight).

Belgian Gay & Lesbian Pride (www.pride.be; ☺ Sat in May) culminates in this area with a vast all-night party. The **Festival du Film Gay & Lesbien de Bruxelles** (www.fglb.org; ☺ late Jan/early Feb.) runs for 10 days in late January, and Cinéma Nova runs occasional **Pink Screen Weeks** (www.gdac.org).

Handily central gay-friendly accommodation includes **Downtown-BXL** (☏ 0475 29 07 21; www.downtownbxl.com; Rue du Marché au Charbon 118-120; d €109-119; ☏; ▣ Anneessens), well placed for the nightlife area.

Money

Credit cards are accepted in almost all hotels and restaurants.

In Bruges, find ATMs at the central **post office** (☏ 050-33 14 11; www.bepost.be; Smedenstraat 57; ☺ 9am-6pm), an ATM at Simon Stevinplein 3 in the Markt, and generally wherever there's a Europabank sign.

In Brussels, ATMs can also be found throughout the city. Find exchange facilities near the Bourse, at Bruxelles-Midi station and at Brussels Airport.

It is not customary to tip in Belgium, but if you feel the need to do so, generally 10% is more than enough. In tourist-oriented locations, unaware foreigners regularly leave disproportionate tips, leading to a certain expectation from staff. Airport taxi drivers may hint (or even state outright) that a tip is appropriate. But that's a gentle scam. Don't be bullied.

Public Holidays

New Year's Day 1 January

Easter Monday March/April

Labour Day 1 May

Iris Day 8 May

Ascension Day 39 days after Easter Sunday (always a Thursday)

Pentecost Monday 50 days after Easter Sunday

Belgium National Day 21 July

Assumption Day 15 August

All Saints' Day 1 November

Armistice Day 11 November

Christmas Day 25 December

Safe Travel

Bruges is a safe city with a low crime rate. It's generally safe (and delightful) to stroll around after dark, but as with all major cities, use your common sense. Pickpocketing can always be a

Dos & Don'ts

Say hello, wave goodbye When entering a shop or arriving at a cash desk, it's polite to offer a cheery greeting to staff. And as you leave say thank you and good day/good evening (in French using the specific terms *bonne journée/bonne soirée*).

Giving gifts When visiting someone's home, it's appropriate to bring wine, flowers or chocolates – choose the brand carefully!

Liberal or conservative? Local ideas about political correctness might not match your own. Don't be too quick to jump to conclusions. A lighter-hearted approach to serious issues is common, and underneath, many attitudes are very liberal.

Kissing Traditionally Belgians welcome good friends with three kisses on alternating cheeks. But knowing when that's appropriate confuses even the locals.

problem in crowded public squares.

The crime rate is low in Brussels compared to other European capitals. Pickpocket haunts include around the Grand Place, Rue Neuve and the markets at Gare du Midi and Place du Jeu-de-Balle. Avoid parks at night.

Telephone services

Most EU mobile phone contracts allow customers roaming in Belgium as though they were in their home country. For non-EU visitors, the cheapest and most practical solution is usually to purchase a local SIM card for your GSM phone, though do make sure your phone isn't blocked from doing this by your home network. There are several providers.

Toilets

o Public toilets are generally clean and well looked after.

o You're expected to tip the attendant around €0.50.

Tourist Information

There are three main locations in Bruges. Each dispenses a bunch of free stuff, sells guide booklets and city maps, and offers local advice, although staff can seem quite exhausted from all the questions during peak periods, so have patience.

You should also be able to get your hands on the excellent local Use-it map/guide (www.use-it.be), but if they're not in stock, browse online.

Tourist Information Counter (☎ 050-44 46 46; www.visitbruges.be; Stationsplein; ⊙10am-5pm Mon-Fri, to 2pm Sat & Sun)

Tourist Office (In&Uit Brugge) (Map p64, B3; ☎ 050-44 46 46; www.visitbruges.be; Concertgebouw, Het Zand 34; ⊙10am-5pm Mon-Sat, 10am-2pm Sun)

Markt (Historium) InfoKantoor (Map p42, D3; ☎ 050-44 46 46; Markt 1; ⊙10am-5pm)

Brussels information:

BIP (Map p112, F2; ☑ 02-563 63 99; http://bip.brussels/en; Rue Royale 2-4; ⊙ 9.30am-5.30pm Mon-Fri, 10am-6pm Sat & Sun; Ⓜ Parc) Helpful Brussels area tourist office.

Flanders Info (Map p84, E4; ☑ 02-504 03 00; www.visitflanders.com; Rue du Marché aux Herbes 61; ⊙ 9am-6pm Mon-Sat, 10am-5pm Sun; 🔊; 🚇 Bourse) The low down on the Flanders region.

Tourist Information Booth (⊙ 8am-8pm; Ⓜ Gare du Midi) Handy information booth if you're at Gare du Midi.

Use-It (☑ 02-218 39 06; www.brussels.use-it. travel; Galerie Ravenstein 17; ⊙ 10am-6pm Mon-Sat; 🔊; Ⓜ Gare Central) Very welcoming youth-oriented office with a list of nightly events, great maps and a free city tour.

visit.brussels

(☑ 02-513 89 40; www.visit.brussels; Hôtel de Ville, Grand Place; ⊙ 9am-6pm; 🚇 Bourse) High-quality information and hand-outs, with an additional office on Rue Royale, where you'll also find the **Arsène50 desk** (www.arsene50.be; Rue Royale 2; ⊙ 12.30-5pm; Ⓜ Parc).

Visas

A valid passport or EU identity card is required to enter Bel-gium. Most Western nationals don't need a tourist visa for stays of less than three months. Those from South Africa, India and China, however, are among those who need a Schengen visa. For more information contact the nearest Belgian embassy or consulate, or check http://diplomatie.belgium.be.

Australian and New Zealand citizens aged between 18 and 30 can apply for a 12-month working holiday visa under a reciprocal agreement – contact the Belgian embassy in your home country.

Language

Belgium is split into Dutch-speaking Flanders (*Vlaanderen* in Dutch) and French-speaking Wallonia (*la Wallonie* in French), as well as a small German-speaking region.

Bruges is Flemish and therefore Dutch-speaking. Brussels is officially bilingual, though French has long been the city's dominant language.

Most of the sounds used in French and Dutch can be found in English. If you read our pronunciation guides below as if they were English, you'll be understood just fine.

To enhance your trip with a phrasebook, visit **lonelyplanet.com**. Lonely Planet iPhone phrasebooks are available through the Apple App store.

French

Basics

Hello.
Bonjour.   bon·zhoor

Goodbye.
Au revoir.   o·rer·vwa

How are you?
Comment   ko·mon
allez-vous?   ta·lay·voo

I'm fine, thanks.
Bien, merci.   byun mair·see

Please.
S'il vous plaît.   seel voo play

Thank you.
Merci.   mair·see

Excuse me.
Excusez-moi.   ek·skew·zay·mwa

Sorry.
Pardon.   par·don

Yes./No.
Oui./Non.   wee/non

Do you speak English?
Parlez-vous   par·lay·voo
anglais?   ong·glay

I don't understand.
Je ne comprends   zher ner
pas   kom·pron pa

Eating & Drinking

A coffee, please.
Un café,   ewn ka·fay
s'il vous plaît   seel voo play

I'm a vegetarian.
Je suis   zher swee
végétarien/   vay·zhay·ta·ryun/
végétarienne. (m/f)   vay·zhay·ta·ryen

Cheers!
Santé!   son·tay

That was delicious.
C'était délicieux!   say·tay
   day·lee·syer

Please bring the bill.
L'addition,   la·dee·syon
s'il vous plaît.   seel voo play

Shopping

I'd like to buy ...
Je voudrais   zher voo·dray
acheter ...   ash·tay ...

I'm just looking.
Je regarde.   zher rer·gard

How much is it?
C'est combien?
say kom·byun

It's too expensive.
C'est trop cher.
say tro shair

Can you lower the price?
Vous pouvez baisser le prix?
voo poo·vay bay·say ler pree

Emergencies

Help!
Au secours!   o skoor

Call the police!
Appelez la police!
a·play la po·lees

Call a doctor!
Appelez un   a·play un médecin!   mayd·sun

I'm sick.
Je suis   zher swee malade.   ma·lad

I'm lost.
Je suis perdu/perdue. (m/f)
zhe swee·pair·dew

Where are the toilets?
Où sont les   oo son lay toilettes?   twa·let

Time & Numbers

What time is it?
Quelle heure   kel er est-il?   ay til

It's (eight) o'clock.
Il est (huit)   il ay (weet) heures.   er

It's half past (10).
Il est (dix) heures et demie.
il ay (deez) er ay day·mee

morning	*matin*	ma·tun
afternoon	*après-midi*	a·pray·mee·dee
evening	*soir*	swar
yesterday	*hier*	yair
today	*aujourd'hui*	o·zhoor·dwee
tomorrow	*demain*	der·mun
Monday	*lundi*	lun·dee
Tuesday	*mardi*	mar·dee
Wednesday	*mercredi*	mair·krer·dee
Thursday	*jeudi*	zher·dee
Friday	*vendredi*	von·drer·dee
Saturday	*samedi*	sam·dee
Sunday	*dimanche*	dee·monsh

1	*un*	un
2	*deux*	der
3	*trois*	trwa
4	*quatre*	ka·tre
5	*cinq*	sungk
6	*six*	sees
7	*sept*	set
8	*huit*	weet
9	*neuf*	nerf
10	*dix*	dees
100	*cent*	son
1000	*mille*	meel

Transport & Directions

Where's ...?
Où est ...?   oo ay ...

What's the address?
Quelle est l'adresse?
kel ay la·dres

Can you show me (on the map)?
Pouvez-vous m'indiquer (sur la carte)?
poo·vay·voo mun·dee·kay (sewr la kart)

I want to go to ...
Je voudrais aller à ...
zher voo·dray a·lay a ...

What time does it leave?
À quelle heure est-ce qu'il part?
a kel er es kil par

Dutch

Basics

Hello.
Dag./Hallo.
dakh/ha·loh

Goodbye.
Dag.   dakh

How are you?
Hoe gaat het met u?
hoo khaat huht met ew

Fine. And you?
Goed. En met u?
khoot en met ew

Please.
Alstublieft.
al·stew·bleeft

Thank you.
Dank u.   dangk ew

Excuse me.
Excuseer mij.
eks·kew·zeyr mey

Yes./No.
Ja./Nee.   yaa/ney

Do you speak English?
Spreekt u Engels?
spreykt ew eng·uhls

I don't understand.
Ik begrijp   ik buh·khreyp
het niet.   huht neet

Eating & Drinking

I'd like the menu, please.
Ik wil graag een menu.
ik wil khraakh uhn
me·new

What would you recommend?
Wat kan u aanbevelen?
wat kan ew
aan·buh·vey·luhn

Delicious!
Heerlijk!/Lekker!
heyr·luhk/le·kuhr

Cheers!
Proost!   prohst

Can I have the bill, please?
Mag ik de rekening alstublieft?
makh ik duh
rey·kuh·ning
al·stew·bleeft

breakfast   *ontbijt*
ont·beyt

lunch   *middagmaal*
mi·dakh·maal

dinner   *avondmaal*
aa·vont·maal

beer   *bier*
beer

bread   *brood*
broht

coffee   *koffie*
ko·fee

fish   *vis*
vis

meat   *vlees*
vlays

nuts   *noten*
noh·tuhn

red wine   *rode wijn*
roh·duh
weyn

tea   *thee*
tey

Shopping

I'd like to buy ...
Ik wil graag ... kopen
ik wil khraakh ...
koh·puhn

I'm just looking.
Ik kijk alleen maar.
ik keyk a·leyn maar

How much is it?
Hoeveel kost het?
hoo·veyl kost huht

That's too expensive.
Dat is te duur.
dat is tuh dewr

Can you lower the price?
Kunt u wat van de prijs afdoen?
kunt ew wat van duh
preys af·doon

Do you have any others?
Heeft u nog andere?
heyft ew nokh
an·duh·ruh

Emergencies

Help!
Help!   help

Leave me alone!
Laat me met rust!
laat muh met rust

Call the police!
Bel de politie!
bel duh poh·lee·see

Call a doctor!
Bel een dokter!
bel uhn dok·tuhr

I'm sick.
Ik ben ziek.
ik ben zeek

I'm lost.
Ik ben verdwaald.
ik ben vuhr·dwaalt

Where are the toilets?
Waar zijn de toiletten?
waar zeyn duh
twa·le·tuhn

Time & Numbers

What time is it?
Hoe laat is het?
hoo laat is huht

It's (10) o'clock.
Het is (tien) uur.
huht is (teen) ewr

Half past (10).
Half (elf).   half (elf)
(lit: half eleven)

morning   *'s ochtends*
sokh·tuhns

afternoon   *'s middags*
smi·dakhs

evening   *'s avonds*
saa·vonts

yesterday   *gisteren*
khis·tuh·ruhn

today   *vandaag*
van·daakh

tomorrow   *morgen*
mor·khuhn

Monday   *maandag*
maan·dakh

Tuesday   *dinsdag*
dins·dakh

Wednesday   *woensdag*
woons·dakh

Thursday   *donderdag*
don·duhr·dakh

Friday   *vrijdag*
vrey·dakh

Saturday   *zaterdag*
zaa·tuhr·dakh

Sunday   *zondag*
zon·dakh

1	*één*	eyn
2	*twee*	twey
3	*drie*	dree
4	*vier*	veer
5	*vijf*	veyf
6	*zes*	zes
7	*zeven*	zey·vuhn
8	*acht*	akht
9	*negen*	ney·khuhn
10	*tien*	teen
100	*honderd*	hon·duhrt
1000	*duizend*	döy·zuhnt

Transport & Directions

Where's ...?
Waar is ...?
waar is ...

What's the address?
Wat is het adres?
wat is huht a·dres

Can you show me (on the map)?
Kunt u het mij tonen (op de kaart)?
kunt ew huht mey toh·nuhn (op duh kaart)

Please take me to ...
Breng me alstublieft naar ...
breng muh al·stew·bleeft naar ...

What time does it leave?
Hoe laat vertrekt het?
hoo laat vuhr·trekt huht

A ticket to ..., please.
Een kaartje naar ... graag.
uhn kaar·chuh naar ... khraakh

I'd like to hire a bicycle.
Ik wil graag een fiets huren.
ik wil khraakh uhn feets hew·ruhn

Behind the Scenes

Send Us Your Feedback

We love to hear from travellers – your comments help make our books better. We read every word, and we guarantee that your feedback goes straight to the authors. Visit **lonelyplanet.com/contact** to submit your updates and suggestions.

Note: We may edit, reproduce and incorporate your comments in Lonely Planet products such as guidebooks, websites and digital products, so let us know if you don't want your comments reproduced or your name acknowledged. For a copy of our privacy policy visit lonelyplanet.com/privacy.

Benedict's Thanks

A huge shout out to LPers Daniel Fahey and Tamara Sheward for their patience, trust and guidance. My special thanks to Stefano Marin and my friends in Berlin, Matti, Anna, Robert and Kira for your support; to my brother Andy, to Mum (as always) and the rest of the Walker and Cook clans for your continued encouragement. Dedicated to Warner Cook, Kevin Hennessy and James Ham.

Helena's Thanks

Sincere thanks to Pierre Massart and Gary Divito for the lowdown on Brussels, and to EU expert Andrew Gray. Plus all my friends in Brussels for their advice, ideas and support.

Acknowledgements

Cover photograph: Guild houses, Markt, Bruges, Richard Taylor/4Corners ©
Photographs p32: Olena Z/Predrag Jankovic/Shutterstock ©; p76: telesniuk/trabantos/S-F/Shutterstock ©

This Book

This fourth edition of Lonely Planet's *Pocket Bruges & Brussels* guidebook was curated by Benedict Walker, and researched and written by Benedict and Helena Smith. The previous edition was also written by Helena. This guidebook was produced by the following:

Destination Editor
Daniel Fahey

Senior Product Editors
Grace Dobell, Genna Patterson

Regional Senior Cartographer
Mark Griffiths

Product Editor
Barbara Delissen

Cartographer
Julie Sheridan

Book Designer
Fergal Condon

Assisting Editors Tamara Sheward, Simon Williamson

Cover Researcher
Naomi Parker

Thanks to William Ballantine, Wayne Cardoza, Jennifer Carey, Melanie Dankel, James Smart, Paul Snell, Eldrid Verbeke, Mirjam Zdybel

Index

See also separate subindexes for:

⊗ **Eating p158**
⊘ **Drinking p159**
☼ **Entertainment p159**
🔒 **Shopping p159**

Our Writers

Benedict Walker

A beach baby from Newcastle (Australia), Ben turned 40 in 2017 and decided to start a new life in Leipzig, Germany. Writing for LP was his childhood dream, and it is a privilege, a huge responsibility and loads of fun. Come along for the ride, on Insta! @wordsandjourneys.

Helena Smith

Helena is an award-winning writer and photographer covering travel, outdoors and food – she has written guidebooks on destinations from Fiji to northern Norway. Helena is from Scotland but was partly brought up in Malawi. She also enjoys global travel in her multicultural home area of Hackney and wrote, photographed and published *Inside Hackney,* the first guide to the borough (https://insidehackney.com).

Contributing writer

Mark Elliott contributed to the Survival Guide chapter.

Published by Lonely Planet Global Limited
CRN 554153
4th edition – Apr 2019
ISBN 978 1 78657 380 3
© Lonely Planet 2019   Photographs © as indicated 2019
10 9 8 7 6 5 4 3 2 1
Printed in Malaysia